Legal Handbook for Small Business

Legal Handbook for Small Business

Revised Edition

Marc J. Lane

amacom

American Management Association

This book is available at a special
discount when ordered in bulk quantities.
For information, contact Special Sales Department,
AMACOM, a division of American Management Association,
135 West 50th Street, New York, NY 10020.

Library of Congress Cataloging-in-Publication Data

Lane, Marc J.
    Legal handbook for small business.

    Includes index.
    1. Small business—Law and legislation
—United States.   I. Title.
KF1659.L36   1989   346.73'0652   88-48039
ISBN 0-8144-5951-X   347.306652

First edition © 1977, AMACOM Books

Printing number

10 9 8 7 6 5 4 3 2 1

For
Rochelle,
my wife,
and **Allie, Mandy,** and **Jennifer,**
our daughters, with love.

Table of Contents

Acknowledgments

In the first edition of *Legal Handbook for Small Business,* I acknowledged the not insubstantial contributions of my family and Bee K. Schulman, my secretary, without whom that effort (and so many others, I should say) would have been impossible. I can only reiterate my thanks to and for them.

This revised edition bears the thoughtful and deliberate mark of my associate, James Ozyvort Maland, a talented colleague in whom I place great trust.

Finally, I observe now, as I did then, that I realistically share any praise for the work with my clients, whose successes, it is hoped, will lay the foundation for yours.

MARC J. LANE

November 1988

Preface to the Revised Edition

This is a game plan. It traces your legal decision making from the earliest stage of business awareness through all the operational changes you are likely to meet, and it concludes with positive and negative factors that lead the small enterprise to its ultimate choice: to go public or not.

Along the way, legal decisions are viewed as the third dimension to business decisions, the dimension that makes them real. The law's requirements are shown to be fully compatible with the best, most practical answers to even the hardest dollars-and-cents business choices.

A word of caution: Although this book explores the principal legal opportunities and pitfalls you are apt to encounter as the head of a small business, don't make the mistake of thinking that a book can replace your lawyer. Only he or she can apply all the nitty-gritty legal specifics to your special situation. Only he or she can assess the impact of your state's laws (which, because of their diversity, have generally been excluded from our consideration). And only your lawyer will know the very latest shifts in the wind's direction out of Washington.

In the first edition of *Legal Handbook for Small Business*, it seemed a reasonable undertaking to set out in one small volume all the basic legal information an entrepreneur might need to handle the various contracts, tax, banking, insurance, and other activities and relationships pursued by a new enterprise. Small business was and is the core of the national economy, generating an enormous growth of total goods and services in just the last decade. While no one can criticize the overall quantity and quality, or beneficial contribution, of such growth, the inevitable result is a plethora of new laws and regulations to maintain a balance between the source of supply and the demand for consumption. My objective for this revised edition is thus reformulated and, admittedly, a bit less ambitious than that underlying the first edition. Although I reduced somewhat the loftiness of the ideal to be sought, I did so with the firm intent of enhancing the practical utility of the *Handbook*. This enhancement is sought not only through addressing some very important new topics, but also by adding checklists, forms, and examples to the treatment of continuing issues.

The most obvious change is the addition of an entirely new chapter on protecting corporate officers and directors. As executives at the corporate level are subject to substantial personal liabilities arising out of the course of business, the effort is made in Chapter 11 to explain what the law requires and what steps can be taken to reduce the personal exposure.

The Tax Reform Act of 1986 has changed the basics of much business planning, and made obsolete various strategies set out in the first edition of the *Handbook*. Changes in the text on account of new tax provisions appear in about half the chapters, and may account for up to half of all the present revisions.

The new Regulation D of the Securities and Exchange Commission mandated a major overhaul of what is now Chapter 12, which deals with stock and debt offerings. The Federal Trade Commission promulgated its rule concerning franchising and business opportunity ventures, adding layers of new requirements, which are discussed in section 1.10, on franchising.

Vehicle "lemon" laws and new product safety and liability measures are given their fair share of discussion, including current tips for obtaining adequate insurance protection. Occupational safety, environmental protection, employment discrimination, and a vast array of other new or substantially revised topics are set out with guides and practical suggestions for optimum handling.

I hope you will find the commonsense approach refreshing.

Most legal jargon has been omitted, and the fat-free narratives and meaty checklists that guide your way have been cross-referenced for your ease in research. Surely, you will find the *Handbook* useful as a look-it-up source, but I hope you will find it thoroughly readable and that you won't put it on the shelf until you've gone from cover to cover.

Legal Handbook
for Small
Business

A Word About Lawyers

You're not unusual if you question the role of lawyers in our society or in your life. Perhaps Shakespeare's most celebrated line is the one, "First thing let's do—let's kill all the lawyers." (You probably know the citation, so I'll skip that.)

However, if you're serious about running a business, you will need a legal counsellor's help unless you've been practicing in the relevant fields of law yourself for the recent past. Just "any" counsellor won't do; you need a good lawyer who's up to speed in all the areas pertinent to your business, or even perhaps several lawyers. Chapter 7 lists some key pointers on selecting the right counsellor and putting your relationship with him or her on the right basis.

As you read this book, it would be a good idea to jot down any matters you're not sure of. Some of your questions may seem basic or even trivial, but if you don't get clear explanations when you start talking with your attorney, you should probably reconsider your selection. You have rights as a client, including the right to understand what is important for your business.

If a lawyer is worth his or her salt—Chapter 7 should help you decide whether yours is—he or she will be able to answer you clearly and will respect you all the more for seeking the knowledge you need. Both of you should pull together as one team and as the major part of the solution to the problems of your business.

1 Getting Into Business

Seest thou a man diligent in his business? He shall stand before kings.
—Proverbs

1.01 Where to Begin

Logic might insist that we begin at the beginning, but let's not. We must assume that you are unalterably committed to becoming a truly successful entrepreneur and that your independence is a source of deep personal satisfaction. You enjoy responsibility, inspire confidence in those around you, and think in an organized, rational, yet inventive way.

We must assume, too, that no matter how experienced you are, you will seek and follow good advice. Running a business means dealing with complexities beyond the ken of any one individual; even the "mom and pop" enterprise is a team effort today. From the very beginning, you will confer with your lawyer, your accountant, your banker, and your insurance agent or broker. You will rely on a variety of business information clearinghouses, including your local Chamber of Commerce; trade associations; colleges and universities; government offices at every level; the Small Business Administration (SBA), whose workshops on starting and managing new enterprises consistently earn high praise; the SBA's Service Corps of Retired Executives (SCORE), eager to give on-site managerial advice and training on a cost-only basis; private experts of every discipline; and, believe it or not, even your competition and would-be competition.

While it is well to try and try again, you should quit before you start if you have doubts about the kind of product or service you want to offer or are not certain that you have access to the starting capital your venture will require. Your experience, your education, and your personality will probably determine the general nature of the business soon to be yours. The challenge before you is to shape your business concept into the best commercial future you can.

1.02   Starting From Scratch

At once the trickiest, the riskiest, and perhaps the most rewarding way to get into business is to start your own from the ground up, but be cautious: More than one third of all new ventures fail or are discontinued in their first year; two thirds are out of business within five years.

Any new business poses a major risk for its founder, a risk that needs prior control in the form of product research, market analysis, and profit forecasting, all based on a raft of facts it is your job to learn. The most common types of businesses have the advantage of thousands of forebears whose conquests and defeats have lessons to tell, but less traditional products and services dictate more intensive inquiry before an entrepreneurial commitment can be made. At the bare minimum, you and your attorney will want to study these variables:

▶ *Regulation.* What licensing laws affect your business choice, and can you comply with them? How onerous are applicable consumer protection, environmental, antitrust, and labor laws?

▶ *Risk.* Apart from the inevitable risk of investment capital, what other risks are forseeable, and how easily may they be controlled or insured against?

▶ *Location.* If the business opportunity before you is tied to a given site, is that site intrinsically destined for profit in its cost/rent and real estate tax structure? In its proximity to the source of your supplies and materials and to your defined market? In the population dynamics and attitudes of its community? In its access to prospective employees? In its competitive advantages? In its zoning? In the services it furnishes and the cost of those services—rail, shipping, police and fire protection, electricity and gas, water, sewage, whatever else you might need?

▸ *Taxes.* In addition to federal income taxation, can you afford to pay the applicable state and local income taxes? How about unemployment insurance, Social Security withholding, personal property, occupation (license and franchise), and sales taxes? Does your jurisdiction foster commercial and industrial development through tax incentives or tax holidays? Have you considered possible tax advantages of leasing assets for use in the business from yourself or other family members?

▸ *Capital requirements.* How much will you need to invest before profitability is achieved, months or even years from now? What will your *organizational expenses* be for market survey and investigations, for projections and estimates, for legal and accounting services through the organization of your business structure? Can you reduce the amount of needed capital by leasing property and equipment? What will your *start-up costs* be for initial inventories, supplies, machinery, furniture, and other necessary assets? Can you estimate your profit margin and first-year sales volume and determine the level of *operating expenses* until your projected break-even date, including the cost of replenishing inventories, payrolls, and other routine business expenses?

▸ *Credit.* Will you need to sell on credit or accept credit cards? If deliveries to consumer locations are likely, will you require cash payment before delivery, or will you accept payment by check on ten- or thirty-day terms?

▸ *Distribution.* Will you be able to make deliveries to customer locations by outside agencies such as United Parcel Service, or will you require an in-house distribution capacity? Have you considered indirect delivery costs such as insurance against vehicle operator liabilities and accidental losses?

▶ *Promotion.* What range of expenditures for advertising, Yellow Page listings, direct mail, and other promotional activities do you expect to have?

▶ *Computerization.* Will computer program, telecommunication, and photocopying equipment make your business more efficient in handling billings, payroll, inventory, word processing, delivery, and other activities? Have you considered payroll and fringe benefit costs for the staff to operate such equipment?

▶ *Return.* Ultimately, will your business be likely to pay a better-than-savings-account return on your investment plus reasonable compensation for your efforts?

1.03 The Ideal Purchase

For many, a ground-zero start-up presents an exciting and irresistible challenge. For others, the risks are simply too high. One alternative is to purchase a going concern. With planning, you may benefit from your predecessor's spadework in all these ways:

- ▶ You can bypass the hassle of developing a fuzzy business idea into a product line, a location, a customer base, inventories, employees, and all the rest;
- ▶ You can inherit the goodwill someone else spent years to build;
- ▶ You can forgo the lean years that brand-new businesses invariably struggle through; and
- ▶ With luck, you can pick up a real bargain, especially if you are buying from someone who needs quick cash or just can't wait to retire.

1.04 Your Lawyer's Checkup

Success is rarely easy, and never automatic, even for the prospective purchaser with a blank check. Consistently profitable, troublefree businesses are seldom sold. (Would you sell one if you owned it?)

Be skeptical, and demand strict proof that the venture for sale will form a solid basis for your growth.

Business achievements are the dollars-and-cents product of valuable legal rights. A legally sound enterprise is capable of attaining genuine business success; a legally defective one must be cured at any cost before healthy business growth can commence. For that reason, a critical but objective head-to-toe checkup must be your lawyer's first assignment. The examination he systematically conducts will lay bare the legal reality of the enterprise that interests you.* None of the following significant business elements should escape your attorney's attention:

▶ *Transferability of assets.* See that your lawyer scrutinizes documents of title and public records to confirm that the assets for sale are free of encumbrances and restrictions on use.

▶ *Seller's assistance.* If you are relying on the seller to introduce you to old customers, be sure he makes legally enforceable promises.

▶ *Intellectual property.* Your lawyer should review all trademarks, patents, and copyrights to ensure their legality and scope (see Chapter 4).

▶ *Contractual relations.* He will need to study the rights and obligations under existing contracts, leases, permits, and licenses.

▶ *Securities law compliance.* In the corporate context, your lawyer should trace shareholdings to keep you on the safe side of Securities and Exchange Commission regulations and state blue-sky (securities) laws (see sections 11.08 and 11.09).

▶ *Other governmental regulation.* He will also need to assess the burden of compliance with current and proposed antitrust, environmental, and consumer protection legislation.

▶ *Employees' rights.* Your lawyer should examine the venture's labor obligations in light of the Employee Retirement Income Security Act, the Occupational Safety and Health Act, your state's workers' compensation statute, and other relevant standards. He should check overall employee benefit commit-

---

*The pronoun "he" has been used throughout to avoid awkward sentence construction. Where "he" is used, "she" is equally appropriate.

ments to verify adherence to Treasury and Labor Department pronouncements and to project future costs (see Chapter 9).

▶ *Accounting data.* Your lawyer should rely on an independent analysis by your accountant and integrate the accountant's findings into the "legal audit" process. Accounting conclusions—about the age and turnover of inventories, the age, cost, depreciation and insured value of assets, the age and apparent collectibility of accounts receivable, and so much more—will prove invaluable to you in evaluating the true worth of a business (see Chapter 3).

1.05   The Telltale Twenty

These issues just listed and others worth exploring demand access to legal documentation of virtually every description. Move deliberately, and make no purchase decision until all of the following documents, or genuine photocopies, are made available to you:

1. A list of all states where the seller is incorporated, qualified, or authorized to do business, and the respective inception dates of that authority.
2. Copies of all the seller's patents, trademarks, copyrights, licenses, and any agreements for such rights.
3. All real estate, equipment, and motor vehicle leases to which the seller is a party, whether as lessor or lessee.
4. Deeds to all real estate the seller owns.
5. Titles to all motor vehicles the seller owns.
6. All instruments creating liens, encumbrances, or charges against any of the seller's real or personal property.
7. A list of all banks where the seller maintains accounts and safety deposit boxes, the names of all those with access to them, and comprehensive statements of account provided by such banks.
8. A list of all the seller's securities and cash equivalents such as CDs, Fannie Maes, Ginnie Maes, and Freddie Macs.
9. A list of all outstanding powers of attorney executed by the seller.

10. A list of all the seller's officers and directors (or, if the business is unincorporated, all top-level employees) and their salaries, bonuses, and benefits in the nature of compensation.
11. All employment contracts.
12. All labor union contracts.
13. All stock bonus, stock option, profit-sharing, retirement, and 401(k) plans, and their qualification status, together with any hospitalization, medical reimbursement, and insurance plans.
14. A list of all pensioned employees whose pension benefits are unfunded, and data reflecting whether such pensions have been reduced to a written instrument.
15. A list of all employees who will be eligible to retire within the next five years by reason of any formal or informal company plan or policy.
16. A list of any cease-and-desist orders or injunctions in force, any pending litigation, workers' compensation claims, and discrimination and environmental complaints.
17. Recent profit-and-loss statements and balance sheets, supported by copies of recent federal and state income tax returns and the report of the last Internal Revenue audit.
18. All continuing contracts for the purchase of materials, supplies, and equipment, and all contracts continuing over the next year (except minor, routine sales contracts, purchase orders, subscriptions, and supply contracts).
19. All contracts and pending bids relating to projects over $10,000 (or a lesser sum for smaller businesses).
20. A list of creditors, so that you can determine the difficulties of complying with Article VI of the Uniform Commercial Code (usually called the Bulk Sales Act).

1.06 To Buy or Not to Buy?

Sit down with your attorney and go over the legal data that count. Weigh the deal-breaker factors, the make-it-or-break-it business considerations that will influence your decision to buy or not to buy. If the following questions yield answers that make you squirm, you should probably look elsewhere.

- ▶ *Why is the seller selling?* Are there sound personal reasons, or does a basic flaw compel a sale?
- ▶ *What are the prospects for future growth and profit?* What is your candid assessment of the location, traffic patterns, the new-customer market, reorder or repeat business, the competition?
- ▶ *Are the tangible assets worth buying, or have they deteriorated and become obsolete?* Does the equipment do its job efficiently, or is it outdated? Is the inventory really valuable, or is it a herd of white elephants?
- ▶ *What are the seasons for different kinds of sales?* How do they affect the turnover of inventory on hand?
- ▶ *Can the intangibles generate a profit for you?* What fraction of accounts receivable is worthless? Have any patents, contract rights, or franchises made money in the recent past? If so, are there foreseeable circumstances that might change that profitability?
- ▶ *Can the goodwill really be sold, or is it tied to the personality of the seller?* Will the seller become an employee of yours? Will he sign a noncompetitive agreement? How much ill will offsets the goodwill?
- ▶ *What liabilities might you unwittingly be assuming?* What contingent liabilities can you spot?
- ▶ *How important are the key employees?* Are they happy? Will they remain with the enterprise? Are they replaceable? At what cost?
- ▶ *What operational changes will you require?* What will these improvements cost?
- ▶ *Can you rely on the seller's list of creditors in order to ensure compliance with the Bulk Sales Act?* Without such compliance, you will become obligated under the seller's debts, and even tax and withholding obligations, even though your agreement provides otherwise.

1.07   The Price of Profit

Even if you are satisfied that a business opportunity is ideal and that it's being offered at a low price, its fair market value may be even lower. You and the seller should first determine what method to use in establishing the actual price. Although setting the price usually involves a large measure of old-fashioned horse trading and can get out of hand with difficult calculations, the method to be used should fit the known facts.

Four general methods of determining price are the book-value method, the appraised-value method, the formula valuation method, and the residual method (formerly called the 1920 IRS method), any of which may best fit the facts of your transaction.

Book Value

The book-value method looks to the sum of tangible assets at cost less accumulated depreciation minus liabilities. If the books have been kept on the cash-basis method (section 3.04) and do not carry amounts for accounts receivable or accounts payable, then adjustments should be made to include the net value addition or liability deduction with respect to both of these sets of accounts. If no reserve for income taxes owed on current income or accumulated earnings is reflected on the books and these liabilities will remain with you or the business, further book-value method adjustments are appropriate.

A common arrangement is to use book value as of the end of the accounting period preceding the sale-purchase, adjusting to take into account the time after that period up to the closing. However, even though the book-value method is often used and usually yields the lowest price for the buyer, it generally fails to assign fair value to goodwill, possible appreciation in physical assets and inventory, and the ongoing value of intangibles such as patents and trademarks. The parties may negotiate adjustments for such items, use a different valuation method designed to make such adjustments, or use a blend or average of valuations derived from one or more different methods.

Appraised Value

The appraised-value method is similar to an arbitration. Each party names a professional or other qualified appraiser. If both name the same appraiser, that person's appraisal will establish the price. If the parties name different appraisers, they are limited to the sole function of agreeing on the independent expert who will actually do the appraisal. The availability of expert appraisers in the field of small business has grown significantly, so that the competition among them helps somewhat in reducing their fees.

In order to gain some control over the result of an appraisal, you should provide standards in your agreement for valuations of different categories of assets, with specific directions in various areas such as the following:

- ▶ Using market value, replacement value, insurance value, or book value for real property and equipment
- ▶ Valuing inventory at cost, market, or the lower of cost or market
- ▶ The standard to be used in valuing goodwill

Formula Valuation

The usual formula valuation method is to capitalize average annual earnings for the preceding three or five years by an agreed factor that typically ranges from 3 to 10. Thus, if average after-tax net earnings were $60,000 per year during the agreed measuring period and 5 were the agreed factor, the price of the business would be $300,000. In most cases, the use of this method is adjusted by adding back the owner's before-tax compensation over the measuring period, which compensation the owner received from the business (triggering deductions from the earnings of the business).

If earnings have fluctuated widely, rather than staying fairly constant, it becomes harder to support the application of the theory underlying the formula valuation method to the fact situation. Such theory assumes that it is possible to project into the future the "normal" annual after-tax results. As a result of this difficulty, where there has been substantial earnings fluctuation, parties often average or blend the prices determined using the various basic methods.

Residual or 1920 IRS Method

One "blend" method is the so-called 1920 IRS method, named after an opinion issued in 1920 by the Committee on Appeals and Review of the Bureau of Internal Revenue. This method proceeds as follows:

1. Determine the value of net tangible assets on the basis of the market value of all current and long-term assets less liabilities—this would usually be somewhat more than a valuation according to the book-value method because adjustments are made for market value increases in inventory, plant and equipment, and other tangible assets.
2. Determine the value of intangible assets:
    a. Compute average earnings over the preceding five years by adding all the annual, net after-tax earnings of the business, together with the owner's before-tax compensation from the business for such years and dividing by five.
    b. Calculate the portion of earnings attributable to net tangible assets on the basis of an assumed 8½ percent return on such assets, so that if the value determined in item 1 above were $200,000, then $17,500 would be the earnings deemed to be so attributable.
    c. Calculate the portion of earnings attributable to goodwill by deducting the portion calculated in item 2b from the average earnings determined in item 2a.
    d. Capitalize the portion of earnings deemed to be attributable to goodwill at 15 percent by multiplying the result determined in item 2c by 6⅔ (6.6667).
3. Add the result obtained in item 2d, the capitalized earnings value of intangible assets, to the value of tangible assets determined in item 1 to determine the value of all assets, or the fair price for the business.

If you exclude the 8.5 percent factor and the 15 percent capitalization assumption (the 6.6667 multiplier) from the 1920 IRS method, what is left is essentially the residual method. The Tax Reform Act of 1986 makes the residual method mandatory for both parties in allocating the purchase price among the different assets of a business sold in the current tax year. However, the residual method requires one further adjustment, namely: adding the market value of *incorporeal assets* other than goodwill into the value of tangible assets. In the accounting sense, *incorporeal assets* means franchises, leases, trade names, subscription lists, secret processes, organizational costs, patents, trademarks, and copyrights. (Securities and cash equivalents are considered corporeal.) The accounting distinction between corporeal and incorporeal assets, and the adjustment of adding back the value of incorporeal assets other than goodwill to arrive at the value of tangible assets, should be made consistently in any valuation methods used for determining the purchase price of your business. Securities and cash equivalents being transferred with the business should generally be included at market value or face value, respectively, in determining the amount of tangible assets.

Here is a step-by-step illustration:

(1)	Adjusted market value of the tangible net worth plus intangibles other than goodwill:		$200,000
(2)	Five years' average earnings (with add-backs for owner's compensation):	$ 40,000	
(3)	Less 8.5% of tangible assets, assumed to be annual earnings derived from tangible assets:	− 17,000	
(4)	Balance of average earnings assumed to be derived from goodwill:	23,000	
(5)	Capitalization of earnings derived from goodwill:	× 6.667	± 153,341
(6)	Purchase price [(1) + (5)]		$353,341

Note that the valuation of tangible assets pursuant to the residual method should include, if applicable, the adjustments discussed with respect to the book-value method.

In deriving a reasonable price, also consider the different types of acquisitions available to you. You might purchase corporate stock or a partnership interest, but if so, undisclosed liabilities such as the following could reduce what you think the business is worth:

► A claim for breach of contract or, as exemplified by the famous *Texaco–Pennzoil* case, for interfering with a contractual relationship

► Underpaid past income taxes, with a possible 100 percent in penalties and interest

► Claims for defective products or negligent services (product liability coverage or other insurance may or may not apply, with or without deductible amounts)

► Claims relating to employment discrimination, safety regulations, labor laws, or environmental protection

► Claims or unexpected funding requirements under labor or employment contracts or benefit plans

For many buyers, only the purchase of business assets safeguards the price negotiated by the parties. In an asset acquisition, your contract should allocate the price among the different assets using the so-called residual method in order to comply with the Tax Reform Act of 1986, where the value of goodwill is determined as the excess of the purchase price over the aggregate fair market value of the tangible and intangible assets other than goodwill. Both you and the seller are required to use this method and to provide information about the allocations to the IRS on Form 8594.

Your allocation of the total amount among the various assets will have tax-saving or tax-aggravating consequences, as illustrated in Table 1–1.

1.08 Payment Possibilities

The actual payment of the purchase price need not be COD. Your method of payment should be a creative response to both your needs and those of the seller. Consider these options:

► *An installment purchase.* Make a down payment of part of the total purchase price, with the balance evidenced by a note payable

Table 1-1. Purchase price allocation checklist.

Value these assets relatively high:	Here's why:
Supplies	Their cost is deductible as an expense.
Accounts receivable	To the extent they prove uncollectible, the write-offs are deductible.
Inventories	A high valuation will reduce your taxable profit.
Patents, copyrights, and other intellectual property with a short remaining life	Their cost can be quickly recovered through amortization.
Tangible assets permitted accelerated depreciation	You can deduct their cost even faster than their value to you diminishes (but double-check the alternative minimum tax consequences).
Noncompetition agreement	When contractually severed from goodwill, its cost is deductible ratably over its term.

Value these assets relatively low:	Here's why:
Long-lived tangible assets, ineligible for accelerated depreciation	If you can't write them off rapidly, they simply are not tax favored.
Land	Never wasting away, it's just not depreciable.
Stocks and bonds	Securities aren't depreciable either.
Goodwill	Its cost is recoverable only when you sell your business.

in installments and having at least one installment payable after the close of the tax year in which the sale occurs. The seller's tax gain can usually be spread over a period of years. However, if the seller was a dealer in any of the assets sold, the installment method can't be used for those assets; they should be sold under a separate agreement if the installment method is used for the other assets in which the seller was not a dealer.

▶ *Part purchase, part lease.* Create a tax deduction for your lease payments, and defer much of the seller's taxable gain.

▶ A *contingent payout.* Pay an agreed sum down, with the balance contingent on future earnings. You will be paying for no more than you actually realize, and you can use the cash in the business to pay off the seller.

▶ A *"nonsale."* Take advantage of the seller's brainpower. Keep him on as a partner or participating consultant, or issue notes to him for a portion of the purchase price. Your future success will benefit the seller directly, so you know he will help make your venture profitable.

1.09 Procedural Pointers

Once you and the seller agree about the substance of your transaction, both attorneys will proceed to draft a purchase agreement, spelling out your mutual intent in precise detail. You will notice at least a few safeguards that may never have entered your discussions but will protect your purchase:

▶ Your lawyer should demand compliance with your state's Bulk Sales Act, requiring prior notice of your purchase to all your seller's creditors. That way, creditors will have an opportunity to assert claims against any assets being transferred, and you can take possession without fear of a later challenge to title.

▶ Your lawyer should also verify the extent of any unpaid obligations of the seller for income taxes and withholding, Social Security and unemployment insurance, and sales and use taxes.

Buyers can step into the seller's obligations in these areas by virtue of special provisions for bulk sales pursuant to federal and state laws.

▶ Closing adjustments should be delimited, along with any other liabilities you might be assuming.

▶ The seller's noncompetition agreement should be reasonably defined in time and geographic scope so you can rely on it.

▶ The seller may warrant his legal compliance, his freedom from pending litigation, the absence of any undisclosed liabilities, the validity of his patents, his sole assumption of risk pending the sale's closing, the accuracy of his last balance sheet, the condition of the equipment you are buying—in short, any fact you need to be sure about before you make your purchase commitment. And the seller's warranties will become an *indemnification*, holding you harmless from any damage you might suffer by reason of his breach of warranty.

▶ Your down payment may be held in *escrow* by an impartial third party from whom it can be recovered if the seller fails to perform as promised.

▶ As additional security against an eventual breach, you might have the sale structured so that a part of your purchase price is "held back" until the seller's full performance is satisfactorily completed.

1.10   Franchising: A Happy Hybrid?

Franchising is another alternative for the would-be entrepreneur. It is a system of selective distribution that avoids some of the risks of a new business but still gives you the personal satisfaction of initiating your own venture. A franchise is a license to market a product or service in a standardized, systematized way. It is usually granted in exchange for a set fee, an ongoing percentage of the investor's profits, and the investor's agreement to uphold the standards of the trademark that the franchisor, its owner, may impose. Franchising has enjoyed a veritable explosion. Its appeal is obvious for the following reasons:

- ▶ *Existing goodwill.* You will be dealing in a proven and well-known product or service. It stands to reason that you should get off to a faster start and significantly reduce the risk of failure.
- ▶ *Relatively small capital investment.* The franchisor will have already undertaken substantial steps in research, marketing, and advertising, and you won't be responsible for most of the costs. What's more, the franchise name might well help you attract financing.
- ▶ *Good help from the beginning.* The franchisor may help select your location, negotiate your lease, raise your capital, and supply your equipment and a time-tested design for your physical layout.
- ▶ *Continuing managerial expertise.* At best, you will benefit from all the franchisor's experience. You may be offered management assistance, on-site employee training, inventory control aids, accounting help, and more.
- ▶ *Mass buying power.* A large franchisor can demand volume discounts and pass them along to you.
- ▶ *Wide-area promotion.* The impact of the franchisor's advertising program may do more for you as a small businessperson than you can ever afford to do for yourself.

The Federal Trade Commission's (FTC) "Disclosure Requirements and Prohibitions Concerning Franchising and Business Opportunity Ventures" are intended to make sure that reliable basic information is given to prospective franchisees in a disclosure document and, if earnings claims are made, in an earnings claim document. Many new state laws also apply to franchises located in the respective jurisdictions. In some instances, these laws provide better legal protections than the FTC's rule, depending on the nature of the business and the particular area of franchise relationships. Wrongful terminations, grants of competitive franchises, and very short-term franchises are often restricted under the state laws, whereas the FTC's rule primarily requires disclosures of significant facts.

Losing Control

The advantages of protection and guidance carry with them the big disadvantage of the franchisor's control over the investor. Be sure to ask for documentation to support any projections of earnings, and don't jump at the first opportunity without considering all your alternatives in the same or even other types of business. Although a seasoned operation is usually much safer than a new player, even the most reputable franchise opportunities suffer from these restrictions:

▶ *You will not really be your own boss.* A franchise will be your investment but not your creation. Any franchisor will impose standards and controls that will greatly limit your free will—even your ability to branch out into other lines or to sell your franchise!

▶ *You will share your profits.* After you pay your initial franchise fee, you may be required to pay the franchisor a percentage royalty—forever.

▶ *You will have an uphill bargaining position with the franchisor.* Although the new federal and state laws and regulations provide some legal protections, you and your attorney will be negotiating with a professional staff committed to keeping as much as possible of the franchisor's prerogatives to define territories, settle interfranchise disputes, and control and terminate your operations.

▶ *Buyback promises may not be reliable.* Some state laws prohibit franchisors from making promises to buy back your franchise if annual results don't meet specified amounts: In Ohio, there must be a bond or escrow account to provide security for such a promise.

Evaluating the Franchise Offer

The first step in relating a franchise's pros and cons to your unique requirements is a comprehensive evaluation of the franchise offer. In light of numerous fraudulent "pyramid" promotions, the franchise investor should be asking pointed questions without hesitation. After studying *Franchise Opportunity Handbook*, updated every two years by the U.S. Department of Commerce (available at low cost from Superintendent of Documents, U.S. Government

Printing Office, North Capitol and H Streets, N.W., Washington, D.C. 20402), launch a tough and thorough investigation by addressing the following questions:

▶ *Who is the franchisor?* What is his reputation with his franchisees and the public in general? How long has he been in the business? What is his credit rating? What is his franchise failure rate? (You can write to the International Franchise Association, 1350 New York Avenue, N.W., Washington, D.C. 20005, for a copy of its *Directory of Membership,* which may provide some of the information you need. Other sources to check are the attorney general and the secretary of state in your state.)

▶ *How have other franchisees fared?* Have you contacted as many current franchisees as possible to find out how they've fared and how much support the franchisor has given them? Have you checked *Entrepreneur Magazine,* and especially its annual "Franchising 500" article that lists the most successful current franchises?

▶ *What is the product or service?* Is it well known? Is it competitive? Is it something to be genuinely enthusiastic about? Will the need for it endure? Is it unquestionably legal?

▶ *Where is the market?* What territory would you get and would it be exclusive? Is it adequate? Does it have good growth potential? What competition exists, and what looms ahead?

▶ *Who's got what rights?* Are fees and royalties reasonable? What is your total investment, and what do you get for it? What help will the franchisor give you with raising capital, locating, training, and management? Will you be furnished product liability insurance? Are you permitted to sell the franchise? Are you obligated to carry any new product, or may you opt against one you don't believe in? Do you have the right to renew your contract, or terminate it for good cause? Has the franchisor complied with all state and federal laws? Are you obligated to buy specific volumes of inventory, and can inventory be returned for credit? Is there a requirement to maintain working capital or specified levels of sales? If so, what is the consequence of failing to comply? Will you be required to contribute to an advertising fund? If so, is the amount reasonable, and would you benefit in proportion to your contribution?

▸ *What will the effect be on you?* How much money are you likely to earn? Would you be better off than you would be by starting a business on your own? Do the advantages clearly outweigh the disadvantages? Can you comfortably comply with the franchisor's standards?

A Legal Look at the Franchise Documents

Once you have completed your preliminary evaluation of the franchise offer, have your lawyer dissect the franchise documents to assess the legality of the basic agreement and ascertain the obligations, risks, rights, and liabilities that would be yours. Watch out for these frequently litigated points of potential dispute:

▸ *The degree of control.* The franchisor's legal right to control derives from the Lanham Act, which makes it his duty to "police the trademark" and ensure that product quality and uniformity are maintained. The problem is in defining just how much control is reasonably necessary to police the mark. Too much regulation may be in violation of antitrust laws.

▸ *The true cost of the franchise.* Most agreements will specify a one-time initial fee plus a royalty on a continuing basis. Be sure these are reasonable, particularly if a minimum royalty is established; and note hidden costs, including minimum maintenance standards, advertising contributions, and insurance.

▸ *Pricing.* While a franchisor may suggest prices, he is prohibited from instituting price controls.

▸ *The sources of supply.* The agreement may call for *exclusive dealing*, requiring you, the franchisee, to purchase supplies from the franchisor or another designated source. But you may not be forced to buy items you don't want, nor may the franchisor *tie*, or condition, his sale of one item on your purchase of another unless both products are clearly necessary to protect the quality of the franchise trademark. In general, you should be free to shop for the best products and prices available.

▶ *Advertising.* See that any required contributions to an advertising budget are reasonable and not automatically subject to increases. If you can, reserve some authority in fixing the amount and content of local advertising, and satisfy yourself that contractual advertising policies are aimed at benefiting you.

▶ *Standards and supervision.* Make sure you can live with the requirements. In particular, check the inspection, maintenance, bookkeeping, supervision, and hiring-and-firing provisions. Understand the penalties for violating them.

▶ *The territory.* Be satisfied that the agreement offers you adequate protection against the franchisor's setting up another location too close for comfort. The franchisor may legally restrict himself by protecting your territory, but he may not place restrictions on your legal right to deal noncompetitively anywhere.

▶ *Terminations and nonrenewals.* Working capital requirements and any sales quotas must be reasonable in view of the size, location, and protection of your territory. The franchisor's right to terminate or nonrenew your agreement should be conditioned on good cause and linked to an equitable repurchase procedure. Yet, you deserve both reasonable renewal rights and the right to terminate your agreement with notice; and your interest needs to be protected in the event of your death or disability.

1.11 A Perspective

The major choices are now before you—whether to create a new enterprise, buy an existing one, or operate as the licensee of a parent franchisor. Whichever business concept fits your future, you have already started to recognize that legal decisions and business decisions are inextricably intermeshed. Indeed, one forms the conceptual foundation of the other; and, through your diligence, both will form the foundation of your entrepreneurial success.

2 Structuring the Enterprise

Make good thy standing place, and move the world.

—Goethe

2.01 Following the Form

Even before you open your doors, you will be wise to select a business unit—a sole proprietorship, a partnership, a C corporation, an S corporation, or something else. (The "C" and "S" designations of corporations refer to Subchapters C and S of the Internal Revenue Code, which provide different tax rules for these two categories of corporations.) Sometimes the choice of business form is dictated by external factors: High exposure to legal risks, for instance, may suggest the corporate form with its insulation from personal liability; a tax-sheltering objective may favor a limited partnership. Other times, the business unit is freely selected by a savvy entrepreneur who is acutely sensitive to the legal, tax, and operational results of his decision.

Whatever prompts your selection, know its consequences, and make the most of your choice by maximizing its strengths and mitigating its weaknesses. In particular you should consider the different tax treatments applicable to the alternative ways in which you can operate—go over Exhibit 2–1 with your tax adviser carefully before making any decision.

2.02 Going It Alone

A *sole proprietor* is simply a person who independently conducts an unincorporated business for profit. The proprietorship is created at

24

Exhibit 2-1. A dozen ways to measure different tax treatments.

1 **Taxability of income.** Look at the tax rates, the brackets, and whether you will save by having a separate entity that pays relatively low rates on its first increments of profits.
2 **Deductibility of losses.** Can losses generated by the business be used to offset all other sources of income, just active or passive income, or active and portfolio income? Is the use of losses deferred through a mandatory carryforward?
3 **Organization of the business.** Can assets be transferred to the business without tax? Can the organizational expenses be amortized or written off as deductions against ordinary income without waiting for a liquidation of your interest?
4 **Family planning.** Does the form of the business make it possible to split the income with other family members in order to achieve savings in income, gift, and estate taxes?
5 **Special allocations.** In a group enterprise, can certain individuals receive the benefit of an allocation of a disproportionate amount of income, deductions, or losses?
6 **Fiscal year.** Can the business choose a different fiscal year from that of its owners? If so, can income or loss be accelerated or deferred advantageously as between individual owners and the business?
7 **Fringe benefit deductions.** Are expenses for medical reimbursement plans, group term life insurance, and accident and health insurance plans fully deductible against business income?
8 **Loans.** On loans from the owners, will the business be able to deduct interest against income from all sources? Do the loans increase basis or the amount at risk on the part of the lender-owners in order to provide tax advantages?
9 **Leases.** Will lease rental payments on property leased from owners of the business be deductible against business income from all sources? Can the owners take accelerated depreciation deductions on the leased property?
10 **Liquidation.** Will there be a double layer of taxes on gains upon liquidation, one layer at the level of the business itself and another at the owners' level?
11 **Passive losses.** Can passive losses be deducted in the year they are incurred and against active or portfolio income as well as against passive income?
12 **Alternative minimum tax.** Is the tax position of the business clouded by the book income preference on corporations and other factors relating to the alternative minimum tax?

will without legal documentation. For this reason alone, it is clearly the easiest and cheapest way to start and run a business, and it may be the best way for you to get started. Ordinarily, all one needs to begin operating as a sole proprietor is compliance with local assumed-name and licensing statutes. Since the enterprise has no legal identity apart from its owner, centralized management can be absolute. There are no directors, no officers, and, indeed, no co-owners to impede free-swinging decision making.

Sometimes the price of all this independence can be surprisingly high. Your attorney can help you assess these hidden costs:

▶ A proprietorship leaves you exposed to unlimited personal liability. The business is your alter ego, and judgments entered against it are yours to pay. Of course, you can insure yourself against a multitude of hazards, but some risks are wholly uninsurable, and liability for debts is boundless.

▶ Since a proprietorship is nothing more than its owner, it dies with him, leaving its assets less its liabilities to his heirs. The prospect of the owner's death or incapacity can cloud dealings with would-be creditors, customers, and employees.

▶ Proprietors cannot take advantage of many of the deductible "fringes" enjoyed by corporate shareholder-employees, such as sick-pay plans; medical, dental, and hospitalization plans; medical reimbursement plans; and group term life insurance (see sections 10.01 and 10.03).

▶ In general, tax-planning opportunities are minimal. Inasmuch as the law does not recognize a proprietorship as a distinct entity, the proprietor is taxed on his total business income, whether or not that income is drawn upon for personal use. And taxed income may not be controlled by engineering compensation to the owner. Moreover, a parade of tax deductions are lost to the proprietorship, including the amortization of organizational expenses and the business deduction of passive losses from investments, both of which can create savings for a C corporation.

2.03   Teaming Up

The *general partnership* may offer you greater latitude in business planning. An association of two or more persons to conduct a business for profit as co-owners, the partnership is a legally recognized entity. As such, it offers its owners flexibility in sharing operating responsibilities and decision-making authority. Where partners neglect to negotiate and resolve these issues in front, the Uniform Partnership Act will presume equality in both rights and obligations.

The partnership offers great tax opportunities to the investor. The business is a tax reporter, but not a taxpayer. Every year it files an informational return with the IRS, spelling out each partner's proportionate share of profits, gains, losses, deductions, and credits. Each partner then treats those items as if they were realized or incurred by him directly. The big tax advantage is the partnership's limited ability to allocate income-and-expense items among the owners to achieve the best overall tax result.

In negotiating allocations, note that a partner's share of income is taxed to him even if he does not receive it. Any income retained by the partnership merely increases a partner's tax basis in his partnership interest, reducing his taxable gain upon its ultimate sale. A partner's share of losses (including capital losses) is personally deductible, but he may not deduct more than the *adjusted basis* (before reduction by the current year's losses) of his partnership interest at the end of the partnership year in which the loss is incurred. This adjusted basis is the capital contribution, or the original purchase price, of the partnership interest (less any withdrawals) plus accumulated taxed earnings that have not been withdrawn.

Another tax plus is the partner's privilege to deal with the enterprise as a separate legal entity. He can lease or sell property or loan money to the partnership, all with rather controllable tax consequences.

Even with all these benefits, the general partnership is subject to criticism:

1.   Like the proprietor, the partner is open to unlimited personal liability and, still worse, is liable for the business acts and omissions of his copartners.

2. Any partner can contractually bind the enterprise, since each is its agent. Without a clear-cut agreement, lines of authority can blur, and management by committee can swiftly become no management at all.

3. Under the Uniform Partnership Act, when the partnership agreement does not otherwise provide, a partnership is subject to dissolution at the death or withdrawal of any partner. A new partner can be admitted only with the consent of all the existing partners. Although the termination and admission rules can be varied to some extent by the terms of a partnership agreement, it is still not unusual for a partnership to be subject to an inadvertent termination under the tax laws or to encounter difficulties in transferring interests. The result may be that a partnership looks fragile to potential backers and employees.

Some Partnership Variants

To mitigate the defects just described, new partnership forms have evolved:

▶ *The joint venture*—simply a short-term general partnership created for a limited purpose. Since the venture ends at the conclusion of a specific project, issues of continuity of life and free transferability become moot.

▶ *The limited partnership*—frequently selected for real estate tax shelters. One or more general partners manage the business and remain personally liable for its debts. The other partners are limited in liability to the extent of their investments. They have no rights in management and may transfer their interests (as provided by contract) without dissolving the partnership. Deductible partnership losses are allocated among the general and limited partners in ways designed to maximize offsets against taxable income from the partnership.

▶ *The real estate investment trust (REIT)*—an unincorporated trust or association. It is managed by a trustee for the benefit of 100 or more beneficiaries who currently receive at least 95 percent of the trust's income. REITs enjoy the corporate virtues of continuity of life, free transferability of interests, and centralized management, but are subject to limitations on their ability to retain current after-tax earnings.

▶ *The family partnership*—a device for splitting income among family members to use up zero tax brackets and gain other tax advantages. A high-earnings taxpayer gives a partnership interest in his business, if capital (and not service) is a material income-producing factor, and pays the applicable gift tax. Future income is allocated between the donor (entrepreneur) and donee (family member), allowing reasonable compensation for services rendered to the partnership by the donor, and a lower overall tax liability is possible. However, the donee must also be allocated losses, creating a possible tax detriment if losses do occur. The partnership may not be recognized for tax purposes if the donor (1) has too much control over the distribution of income or assets needed in the business or the sale of a donee's interest, (2) exercises excessive managerial decision making, or (3) does not treat the donee as a partner either in operating or in business relations with the public. Moreover, the compression of tax rate brackets and the "kiddie tax" on minors under age 14 have reduced or nullified the family partnership advantages in many cases. Further, if the donee of a family partnership interest is a minor, such minor, to be recognized as a partner for tax purposes, must be competent to manage his own affairs, and the interest must be held by an adult trustee or guardian—who can be the donor—acting for the sole benefit of the child.

Coming to Terms

The partnership relationship is complex. Don't back away from the controversies that will invariably arise. Instead, opt for candor. Seek out the hot issues and, with your lawyer, bargain for your best position—*before you get into business.* You will have gained all that is rightfully yours, with honor and without the pain of friction among partners. The following issues are worth resolving and reducing to contract form:

▶ *The partnership's name.* Your lawyer will tell you about the legal restrictions that limit your choice and will help you steer clear of any name that is deceptively similar to that of an existing business.

▶ *The nature of the business.* Avoid any conflict in entrepreneurial goals. Since a general partnership obligates you for the business acts and omissions of your copartners, it is wise to limit the scope of your business activities by contract.

▶ *The duration of the partnership.* A partnership can end on a predetermined date, or it can last indefinitely. Either way, a partner might withdraw from the enterprise at any time, without notice, and even in violation of contract, giving rise to his copartners' suit for damages. Since damages may be difficult to value, specify a fair liquidated damages amount, to which you would be entitled upon a partner's premature exit.

▶ *Contributions.* Decide who will contribute what, and when. You may allocate the income from the partnership's eventual sale of a contributed asset to compensate for any difference between its tax basis to the partnership (carried over from the contributing partner) and its fair market value at the time of contribution. Such an arrangement avoids favoring partners who contribute appreciated property.

▶ *Sales, loans, and leases.* To avoid disparities between tax basis and fair market value, you—or any of the partners—can sell your assets to the partnership at their fair market value and individually realize taxable gains and losses. Or you can lend money to the partnership, which can then buy equivalent assets elsewhere; you will realize interest income on your money, deductible by the partnership. A third option: Consider leasing property to your partnership; the partnership can deduct its payments, and your lease income can be reduced by deductible depreciation.

▶ *Distributions and withdrawals.* Unless you agree otherwise, no partner will be entitled to a guaranteed salary from the partnership. Each will be taxed solely on his allocable share of profits less his allocable share of losses, whether or not the difference is actually distributed to him. Spell out the profit-and-loss split in detail, as well as any rights to distributions. Beyond living expenses and personal tax liabilities, you may want to limit both income distributions and capital withdrawals and let the partnership use its money to grow.

▶ *Partners' rights and duties.* Remember that you are legally liable for the acts of the partnership. You have a right to know what the partnership is doing, and you have an obligation to fulfill your decision-making responsibilities. Carefully delineate managerial responsibilities, and set up a settlement procedure to resolve conflicts in judgment.

▶ *Dissolution.* Set out notice requirements for dissolving the partnership and procedures for winding up its business. The partners should agree about the distribution of assets and the payment of liabilities upon dissolution.

▶ *Continuity.* The admission of new partners requires the consent of all existing partners. Agree on consent mechanics and, more important, agree on a "buy-sell" approach. A buy-sell agreement can be a near-perfect answer to the structuring problems arising out of a partner's death. The surviving partners are assured of the right to buy deceased partner's interest, generally with life insurance proceeds, and they retain control of management. The decedent's estate is assured of a fair price (computed by formula), one that will hold up for federal estate tax purposes.

2.04 Why Incorporate?

A *corporation* is the only business structure that is legally recognized as an artificial person. The law's view that a corporation is an entity separate and apart from its owners inescapably leads to the conclusion that it is liable for its own debts and taxes. As you will see, this simple thesis reaps special benefits, such as:

▶ *Insulation from personal liability.* A sole proprietor is liable for all his business debts, and a general partner is responsible for the claims of business creditors when partnership assets do not provide

full coverage, but a shareholder's liability is limited to his investment. And, although shareholders are often called upon to pledge
their personal credit in borrowing business funds, trade creditors
and employees with wage claims cannot reach investors' assets.
Moreover, shareholders are usually shielded from all business tort
liability.

▶ *More favorable tax treatment.* The tax considerations of corporations versus using another form of business entity should be
evaluated in the different ways set out in Exhibit 2-1. Major pro-
corporation factors are the favorable tax treatment that applies to
family gifts of stock, with income-splitting potential, and to qualified benefit plans and the deductibility of premiums for certain insurance programs. And, although top income tax rate brackets may
not be lower for corporations than for individuals, the corporation
as a separate taxpayer begins paying taxes at the lowest rates.
(Professional service corporations, however, are taxed at the high-
est-bracket rates on all income.) Profits not distributed to shareholders—up to $250,000 ($150,000 for service corporations), or
even more—can be accumulated in the corporation, and passive
investment losses can be offset against income from all sources.
When a corporation is formed, the general rule is that no gain or
loss must be recognized by either the corporation or the shareholder, even if assets with appreciation in market value are transferred to the new entity, so long as the transferors control the
corporation—and the same rule enables tax-free transfers of assets
to the entity after it is formed.

▶ *Continuity of business life.* When a proprietor dies, his business may die with him. When a partner dies or withdraws from a
partnership, its business is disrupted and endangered. Yet a corporation may be perpetual, despite the death of an owner or his sale
of shares. That stability alone may be enough to keep employees
feeling secure and creditors calm. What's more, the corporation
offers its owners the greatest range of estate-planning possibilities.

▶ *Centralized management.* All general partners have an equal
voice in decision making, and each is bound by the business acts of

the others. A corporation's shareholders, on the other hand, appoint *directors* to set basic company policy; the directors, in turn, effect that policy through the *officers* they appoint. In small corporations, shareholders, directors, and officers may be the same people. In larger corporations, officers and those they supervise may be structured into their own bureaucracies, or into free-wheeling task forces overlapping organizational lines to solve short-term problems. Simple or complex, the corporation is a decision-making form noteworthy for its systematic delegation of legal responsibilities. One result that is important to you is that liabilities will not ordinarily flow through to the owners.

▶ *Free transferability of interests.* The sale of a partnership interest will not ensure the purchaser's admission to the firm on equal footing with his predecessors; a change in membership requires their prior approval. To convey his interest to a newcomer, a corporate investor needs only to sell his shares and deliver the certificates that represent them. He need not undermine the business or compel its dissolution.

But anticipate some problems: The securities laws may severely restrict transferability, and, even if you are legally able to sell your interest, don't count on a ready market for it. Should you want out, your coshareholders are likely purchasers. Agree in advance about the terms of any eventual buy-out and you'll be sure to receive a fair price.

Where it exists, free transferability is a detriment as often as it is a benefit. If your business is heavily dependent on the rapport the principals have developed, consider a contract to restrict transfers to outsiders.

▶ *Compensation mechanisms.* Since the corporation is the only type of business entity that can issue stock, it is the only way to provide Employee Stock Ownership Plans (ESOPs), Incentive Stock Options (ISOs), other stock options, stock bonus plans, stock purchase plans, stock appreciation rights, or "phantom" stock plans. Often these plans give employees strong growth incentives without necessitating immediate cash outlays.

Against the advantages, you also need to consider a few detriments of the corporate form of business as follows:

▶ *Dividends not deductible.* If the corporation employs the shareholder-owners and pays them reasonable compensation, income tax deductions can be taken by the corporation for those payments, which in a sense can be used instead of dividends as a way to distribute corporate earnings. Thus, the rule that dividends are not deductible often has application only when it becomes necessary to liquidate the corporation—for example, if the owners can neither continue the business nor find any buyer for it. At this point, the nondeductibility rule may necessitate a double layer of taxes on the same income, once at the corporate level in the year earned, and then at the shareholder level when they receive a liquidation distribution.

▶ *Unreasonable compensation.* If family members are on the corporate payroll but do not really earn the amounts they receive as compensation, the compensation will likely be held to be unreasonable for income and gift tax purposes. The result will be the same as if dividends were declared in the amount equal to the excess over a reasonable amount of compensation, with the shareholders receiving taxable income in that amount and also possibly being liable for gift taxes as if the family members were donees of the same amounts—marital, annual, and lifetime exclusions could probably avoid the gift taxes if other gifts were sufficiently limited.

▶ *Piercing the corporate veil.* Courts of law sometimes do not recognize the corporation's limited liability insulation on the ground that shareholder-owners manipulated their own affairs and those of the corporation without observing the legal boundaries between them. Thus, putting corporate money in an individual bank account, or vice versa, without documenting a loan or other basis for that type of handling, can have a devastating result, as can other failures to respect the separate identity of the corporation.

▶ *Administrative considerations.* Corporations involve more complex administration than other business entities, with annual reports, shareholder and director meetings, and other requirements, depending on the applicable state corporation law.

Step-by-Step Incorporation

The advantages of incorporating may be impressive, but what does it really take to incorporate? The corporate name is one of formalities, and all of them are meaningful. If your situation justifies the time and expense, your lawyer will guide you through these steps:

1. *Execute certain contracts.* You and your fellow investors will sign a comprehensive *subscription agreement*, setting out the purpose and structure of the new corporation, your agreement to contribute assets and their value, and the proposed distribution of corporate stock and notes. You will also sign *employment agreements*, detailing the duties and rights of shareholder-employees, including their compensation. In addition, you will probably sign a *buy-sell agreement* restricting the sale of shares to outsiders and obligating the corporation or its shareholders to buy the stock of a deceased shareholder on the basis of a prescribed formula, typically with life insurance proceeds.

2. *Pick a state.* Normally the state in which you will operate is the state in which to incorporate. If you contemplate interstate activities or a fancy debt-and-equity mix, you might consider Delaware or a state having a Delaware-type corporation law. Exhibit 2-2 will tell you why.

3. *Request IRS rulings on any questionable tax aspects of your incorporation.* Especially when you incorporate an existing business, it may be a good idea to seek a Treasury Department opinion of your transaction before it's consummated. The Internal Revenue Code philosophy is to recognize no taxable event in the incorporation of a going concern when incorporators transfer their business assets to the new corporation, receive stock or securities in exchange, and retain control; but be safe.

4. *Draft the charter—the Articles of Incorporation.* Once filed, they will become the corporation's governing instrument.

Exhibit 2-2. Ten good reasons to pick Delaware (or a state with a Delaware-type corporation law).

1 There is no corporate income tax in Delaware for companies doing no business there, no tax on shares held by nonresidents, and no inheritance tax on nonresident shareholders.

2 The private property of shareholders is protected from liability for corporate debts (shareholders' liability is limited to their stock investment), and officers and directors may be indemnified.

3 Shareholders and directors may meet outside Delaware, or meet by conference telephone calls, and keep corporate books and records outside the state.

4 Only one incorporator is required, and that incorporator may itself be a corporation.

5 A Delaware corporation may be perpetual, and it can operate through voting trusts and shareholder voting agreements.

6 Directors may make and alter bylaws, and they may act by unanimous written consent in lieu of formal meetings.

7 Delaware has no minimum capital requirements. A corporation may issue shares—common and preferred, even in serial classes—without par value, fully paid, and nonassessable, for consideration or at a price fixed by the directors. And the directors' judgment about the value of the property or services is conclusive. They may determine what portion of the consideration received goes to capital and what part to surplus.

8 A Delaware corporation can hold the securities of other corporations and all kinds of other property, both in Delaware and outside the state, without limit. It can also purchase its own stock and hold, sell, or transfer it.

9 Any different kinds of business can be conducted in combination.

10 Dividends can be paid out of profits as well as out of surplus.

5. *Hold a shareholders meeting at once, and at least annually thereafter.* The first meeting will see the directors elected.

6. *Hold the first directors meeting* to elect officers; to adopt the bylaws (the rules of internal management); and to approve the corporate seal, the stock certificates (and their issuance), the transfer of property, and the opening of the corporate bank account. The directors will conduct the affairs of the corporation at frequently held meetings. Both shareholders and directors meetings should be recorded by minutes, or you will be hard-pressed to prove they ever happened.

7. *Issue stock.* The directors have OKd the corporation's issuance of stock as provided in the subscription agreement. The actual sale or distribution of corporate stock is regulated by both the states and the federal government. Most initial issues will qualify for an exemption from registration (see sections 11.08 and 11.09). Be sure yours does. In any case, the twin principles of fair dealing and full disclosure must characterize your sale.

When issuing stock, consider an election under Section 1244 of the Internal Revenue Code. That election protects your right to an ordinary loss deduction should the stock become worthless, but you need to consult with your tax adviser as to possible advantages, and the method to use, in so electing.

8. *Order a corporate taxpayer ID number* from the IRS and file consents at once if you are electing Subchapter S status.

S Corporations

Subchapter S of the Internal Revenue Code allows certain small corporations to be taxed much as partnerships are, allowing them to enjoy the advantages of the corporate from without incurring income tax liability at the corporate level. During its early, lean years, a corporation may make the Subchapter S election, permitting business losses to flow through to its owners and, at the same time, preserving the benefits of corporateness. These are the requirements for the S election:

1. At the outset, the corporation must have no more than thirty-five shareholders. (A husband and wife are considered one shareholder if their stock is held jointly.)
2. Individuals, estates, or certain types of trusts must own all the stock.
3. Citizens or resident aliens must own all the stock.
4. It must be a domestic corporation and not a member of an affiliated group eligible to file a consolidated tax return.
5. The corporation must have only one class of stock, but differences in voting rights are allowed.

S Corporation Pluses and Minuses

Subchapter S is not for everyone, but if the foregoing tests are met, some advantages may be available but possibly subject to even greater detriments. The determining factors will usually be the considerations of whether the corporation is expected to be profitable in its first years, levels of compensation to shareholder-employees, the different rates of tax on retained and distributed earnings, and the deductibility of payments for fringe benefits. Arrange a meeting with your lawyer and exchange these ideas:

▶ *Tax rates and brackets.* An S corporation flows its net income through to shareholders, and the only taxes are those of the individuals, usually at slightly lower rates than those applicable to C corporations. However, while top-rate brackets may be higher for C corporations than for individuals, a C corporation as a separate tax entity can usually provide some rate reduction for the first-bracket levels of its earnings.

▶ *Use of losses.* If a corporation is expected to have net losses from operations (other than from passive investments) in its first years, the S election permits those losses to pass through to shareholder-employees, who, if they have materially participated in running the business, can then deduct the losses against income from other sources. However, if the losses were passive at the corporate level or derived from passive-type investments, then the losses can be so deducted only against passive income, notwithstanding the material participation of the shareholder in the S corporation. Moreover, the flow-through losses are deductible only to the extent of the shareholder's basis in stock or debt of the S corporation, and there is a special limit on the deductibility of losses derived from expensing certain depreciable assets. And, the pass-through of losses reduces the shareholder's basis in his stock, creating the potential for later taxes on any future gains. Frequently, for corporations expecting first-year losses, an S corporation election is initially advantageous, but after a year or so, a revocation of the election is indicated, either because net profits are achieved or the limits on loss deductions kick in.

▶ *Effect of losses on stock basis.* While the flow-through of losses in an S corporation results in a reduction of the shareholders' stock basis, that effect can be overcome if the shareholders hold their stock until death, at which point a step-up in basis to the then-current market value is permitted. In the event one or more shareholders expects to sell his stock, however, precise financial calculations will probably be necessary in order to assess the merit of the S election.

▶ *Fringe benefits.* A partner is not an employee for tax purposes and is not eligible for some of the fringes that corporate owner-employees, including S corporation owner-employees, enjoy (see section 10.01 on "Perks"). On the other hand, the costs of some S corporation fringes for shareholder-employees who own more than 2 percent of its stock may not be deductible, even though they would be deductible if paid by a C corporation.

▶ *Loans.* The amount of partnership loss a partner may personally deduct is generally limited to the cost of his partnership interest plus his pro rata share of partnership liabilities. His loans to the partnership increase the partner's basis for absorbing losses only by his share of the liability. In contrast, an S corporation shareholder may deduct his share of the corporate net operating loss up to the cost of his stock plus any corporate debt to him. Therefore, any valid loan from the shareholder to the business directly increases his tax basis for absorbing losses.

▶ *Income recognition.* A partner must report his share of partnership income and losses. If a partnership interest is sold before the year's end, the purchaser earns taxable income from the time of the transfer. S corporation distributions, however, are taxed as dividends in the year the shareholder receives them. Any taxable income remaining in the corporation is taxed to the shareholder in his tax year within the corporation's tax year (or in the year in which the corporation's tax year ends). Such "undistributed taxable income" is shared by those shareholders who own stock on the last day of the corporation's tax year, so S corporation shareholders can redistribute income among themselves or to new owners through the use of good-faith year-end stock transfers.

▶ *Tax year.* In general, neither S corporations nor partnerships can elect to use a taxable year that is different from that of their owners (see section 3.03). C corporations that are not professional service corporations are not so restricted, providing opportunities for acceleration and deferral as to both income and expenses as between the corporate entities and the shareholders.

2.05   Putting It All Together

It should be obvious that your choice of business structure must not be a legal decision by default. Temper overcautious legal thinking with goal-directed business thinking. Insist that your lawyer appreciate your entrepreneurial objectives and that he pragmatically relate them, in detail and in depth, to the law's newest quirks.

3 Tallying Your Profits

It is a socialist idea that making profits is a vice. I consider the real vice is making losses.

—Winston Churchill

3.01 Setting Goals

The orderly recordation, summarization, and analysis of your enterprise's financial data will tell you where your business is prospering, where it is not, and why. No wonder the tailoring of an accounting system to suit your special needs is a prerequisite to controlled business growth. In defining your accounting objectives, consider this advice:

1. *Choose your accountant with care and give him your trust* (see section 7.03). Whether you retain an independent CPA or hire your own controller, make sure he thoroughly understands your business and its policies. An accountant cannot be expected to develop or implement the best system for you without a basic appreciation of who you are and what you are trying to do. Once the two of you have established rapport, level with him; he cannot be legally responsible for any erroneous business impressions you may have given him.

2. *Don't overkill.* All accounting work must generate information of special value to someone—you and your co-owners, the IRS, or your creditors. Any report or subsystem failing to meet that acid test should be dropped pronto. No record is eternally valuable to anyone. From time to time, purge what no longer serves a pur-

pose, and you will gain surer access to the reports you still find meaningful. Exhibit 3-1 is a good throw-it-out-already checklist.

3.02   Financial Accounting vs. Tax Accounting

Understand from the beginning that your accounting system should be functionally responsive. Pure business decisions will be rendered on the basis of the economic conclusions your *financial accounting* subsystem generates. Pure tax decisions will be made only after reviewing information colored by tax notions and derived from your *tax accounting* subsystem. Mixed business-and-tax decisions—as many, if not most, will be—will require study from both perspectives.

The IRS recognizes the desirability of maintaining two inconsistent sets of data. When reviewing your accountant's reports, learn whether he is submitting a financial officer's report or a tax-slanted, but equally legitimate, tax accountant's report. Here are a few of the differences:

▸ Some real income, such as interest on municipal bonds, is excluded from all tax calculations other than the corporate alternative minimum tax (AMT).

▸ Some deductions, including bad debts and casualty losses, may be subject to greater restrictions under tax accounting concepts.

▸ Some income—particularly prepaid income—and some deductions—such as depreciation (section 3.07)—may be reported in different years or in different ways under the two subsystems.

▸ Some special tax deductions—among them the *percentage depletion allowance*, by which the owner of a well or a mine may recover the cost of oil or minerals during the period in which they are extracted—may not represent true cost deductions for financial accounting purposes.

▸ The tax provisions net operating loss carrybacks and carryfor-

Exhibit 3-1. A record-retention checklist.

GENERAL AND FINANCIAL

Capital stock records	Permanent
Bond records	Permanent
Corporate records and minutes	Permanent
Titles and mortgages	Permanent
Expired contracts and agreements	7 years
Year-end general ledgers and trial balances	Permanent
Records of canceled securities	7 years
Insurance records	
Fidelity bonds	3 years
Inspectors reports	Permanent
Schedules and claims	7 years
Expired fire, liability, auto, and other policies	Optional
Record of policies in force	3 years
Federal and state tax records and returns	Permanent
Records of fixed assets and appraisals	Permanent
Accountants' audit reports	Permanent

SALES AND RECEIVABLES

Accounts receivable ledgers	7 years
Accounts receivable trial balances	3 years
Sales journals	7 years
Copies of invoices	3 years
Ratings and investigations of customers	3 years
Uncollectible accounts files, including authorizations for write-off	7 years
Expired contracts with customers	7 years
Records relating to sales to affiliated companies	7 years
Canceled notes receivable and trial balances	7 years
Shipping tickets	3 years

PAYROLLS

Payroll journals and summaries	7 years
Receipted paychecks and time cards	7 years
Payroll deductions records	7 years
Assignments, attachments, and garnishments	3 years
Individual earnings records	Permanent
W-2 forms	3 years
W-4 forms	Permanent

(continued)

Exhibit 3-1. *Continued*

CASH AND COLLECTIONS

Cash receipts and disbursements	Permanent
Bank deposit slips	1 year
Deposit books and stubs	7 years
Bank reconcilement papers	1 year
Records of outstanding checks	7 years
Periodic cash reports	3 years
Canceled checks	Permanent
Canceled payroll checks	7 years
Bank statements (after audit)	7 years
Petty cash vouchers	3 years

INVENTORIES

General inventory with adjustment records	Permanent
Material ledgers (perpetual inventory records)	Permanent
Stores requisitions	3 years
Physical inventory records	3 years

PURCHASES AND PAYABLES

Accounts payable ledgers	7 years
Accounts payable trial balances	3 years
Voucher registers or purchase journals	Permanent
Paid bills and vouchers	7 years
Copies of purchase orders	3 years
Bids and offers	7 years
Price records of purchases	Permanent
Purchase contracts	7 years
Bills of lading	3 years

MISCELLANY

Correspondence	
Legal and important matters	Permanent
General	1–5 years
Interim financial statements	Permanent
Social Security returns	Permanent
State sales tax	Permanent
Federal excise tax	Permanent
Monthly trial balances	5 years
Equipment records	Permanent
Expired leases	7 years

wards will produce widely diverse results between the two subsystems.

▶ More and more accountants insist that financial statements
should be adjusted for the effects of inflation. Some subscribe
to a "purchasing power" approach, adjusting all nonmonetary
items, including inventories, by an inflation index. Others
record assets (and even liabilities) at market prices or replacement value.

3.03 Starting the Year Off Right

A prime function of tax accounting is the computation of taxable
income over a fixed period, usually twelve months, known as a *taxable year*. Both the tax laws and generally accepted accounting
principles require that the accounting system for your business and
the year in which it operates accurately reflect your business profit
profile without distortion. Within these constraints, it may be possible to select a taxable year for your business that is not the same
as your personal tax year. Proprietorships, partnerships, and S corporations are required to use the same taxable years that a majority
of their owners use, unless they can establish to the satisfaction of
the IRS a business purpose for using different taxable years. The
IRS disapproves of the reasons given in most requests for different
taxable years, so that in general, C corporations alone among the
various types of business organizations have a clear path open to the
benefits of having different taxable years at the business and owner
levels, respectively. With proper timing, income and expense items
of C corporations can be accelerated or deferred to engineer favorable tax and cash-flow consequences.

Here are the most common taxable years:

1. *The calendar year.* January 1 through December 31 is the
   natural choice of most small-business owners, but it is not
   always the wisest choice. Should you fail to maintain adequate accounting records, the calendar year will automatically be elected for you.

2. *A fiscal year.* This ends on the last day of a month other than December. A C corporation can split its peak season between two taxable years to spread and partially defer its tax burdens. A new C corporation can end its initial taxable year in fewer than twelve months to defer income and postpone the payment of taxes until the business has survived its first critical year.

3. *A 52-53–week year.* By this variant of the fiscal year, you may use an annual accounting period of 52 or 53 weeks, always ending on the same day of the week. Businesses with weekly income cycles might find the 52-53–week year most appropriate.

3.04   Timing Your Debits and Credits

Once your time frame has been determined, the choice of an accounting method, such as the *cash method* or the *accrual method*, is the biggest accounting decision before you. However, for tax purposes, there are a number of rules that apply to such choice.

In general, the tax rules require that the accrual method of accounting be used by *large* C corporations (other than *personal service corporations*), *large* partnerships that have a C corporation as a partner, certain trusts, and most tax shelters. A *large* C corporation or partnership, in this context, is one with average annual gross receipts of $5 million or more for the three prior tax years, or the period of its existence if less. A *personal service corporation* is a corporation, 95 percent or more of the stock of which is owned by employees rendering services in such fields as health, law, engineering, architecture, accounting, actuarial science, performing arts, and consulting (including but not limited to financial planning).

However, the tax rules require use of the cash method if your business records reflect only cash transactions and there are no inventories.

A taxpayer ordinarily cannot change his method of accounting as a matter of right, so give your selection due consideration at the outset. In practice, these methods operate as follows:

1. The *cash method* records income when it is "constructively" received (that is, available for your use), and deducts expenses when they are paid, unless their deduction at some other time (as is the case of prepaid expenses) would more accurately reflect income. The cash method has the advantage of simple bookkeeping requirements. What's more, it offers the taxpayer an opportunity to defer the receipt of income, to accelerate the payment of expenses, and thus to reduce taxable profit at year-end.

2. The *accrual method* records income when all preconditions to your right to receive it have taken place, even if the money is not yet in your hands. Expenses accrue when their amounts are reasonably certain and you become liable to pay them. The accrual method realistically matches income and expense items with business events as they occur.

3. Various hybrid methods combine elements of both the cash and accrual methods—for purposes of the tax rules just referred to, these hybrids are all considered the same as the cash method. All businesses with inventories must use the accrual method to record purchases and sales, but may, if the tax rules otherwise permit, report other transactions on a cash basis. Subject to such rules, a taxpayer who is involved in more than one activity may adopt the cash basis for some enterprises, the accrual method for others.

4. Special accounting methods may, with some restrictions under the tax laws, be used by cash- or accrual-basis taxpayers to reduce the tax burden resulting from installment sales and long-term construction contracts. However, dealers in personal or real property are not allowed to use the installment method for reporting gains from the sale of such property, and long-term contracts permit only the percentage-of-completion or the percentage-of-completion/capitalized cost methods to be used. The entry of transactions in your journals of account is the concrete application of your accounting method to the financial facts of your business. From these journals, financial statements are created to describe the economic status of your operation, the profit pattern it enjoys, and the allocation of profit among the owners of the business.

3.05   A Delicate Balance

Whatever accounting method you use, the principal output of your system will be three integrated reports: the balance sheet, the income statement, and the statement of owners' equity. The *balance sheet*, which is sometimes called the *statement of financial condition* or the *position statement*, recites the familiar equation:

$$\text{Assets} - \text{liabilities} = \text{owners' equity}$$

This clear interrelationship of accounting components graphically demonstrates that your creditors have claims against the assets of your business and that your rights as an owner are only residual. Exhibit 3-2 is a simplified, but real-life, balance sheet. Let's examine it very closely and see what it really means.

3.06   Summing Up Your Assets

Assets are everything the business owns—real estate, personalty, even intangibles. Balance sheets always divide assets into categories. See how they look in Exhibit 3-2.

Current assets (a) are *liquid assets*, such as cash on hand (b), accounts receivable (c), and inventories (d).

Other assets (e) include *intangible assets* the business has acquired—such as organizational expense, patents, copyrights, and goodwill—and *fixed assets* or *capital assets* (f)—that is, buildings, land, machinery, and any other tangible business property with a useful life in excess of one year (except stock in trade).

3.07   How Depreciation Works for You

For tax purposes, the cost of most intangibles may be deducted or amortized over a period of years. Similarly, capital assets (but not inventories, land, or stock in trade) are generally subject to *depreciation*, an allocation of their cost over the anticipated term of useful life. A reserve for accumulated depreciation is deducted from

Exhibit 3-2. Statement of financial condition.

WHAT-A-COMPANY
Statement of Financial Condition as of December 31, 19x3

(a) *Current assets:*	
(b) Cash and marketable securities	$ 9,480
(c) Accounts receivable	
(Less allowance for doubtful accounts: $1,500)	108,725
(d) Inventories	157,550
Prepaid expenses	4,575
Total current assets	280,250
(g) *Less current liabilities:*	
(h) Notes payable and current portion of long-term debt	31,115
Accounts payable and accrued expenses	59,090
U.S. and foreign income taxes	13,285
Total current liabilities	103,490
(i) *Working capital*	176,760
(e) *Other assets:*	
(f) Property, plant and equipment	141,120
Deferred charges	10,395
Excess of investment in subsidiaries over book value of net assets	28,810
Total other assets	180,325
Assets less current liabilities	357,085
(j) *Less other liabilities:*	
(k) Long-term debt	99,615
(l) Deferred taxes on income and other credits	4,700
Other liabilities	13,000
Total other liabilities	117,315
Excess of assets over liabilities	$239,770
(m) *Shareholders' ownership:*	
What-A-Company shareholders:	
(n) Common stock (authorized, 25,000 shares of $1 par value each; issued, 12,075)	$ 12,075

(continued)

Exhibit 3-2. *Continued*

(o) Excess of shareholders' investment over par value of common stock	32,230
(p) Retained earnings	187,200
	231,505
Less treasury stock at cost (190 shares)	3,265
Total ownership—company shareholders	228,240
Minority interest in subsidiaries	11,530
TOTAL	$239,770

the costs of assets to arrive at the asset value declared on the balance sheet.

In an attempt to standardize depreciation deductions for all taxpayers, the Congress and the IRS have established several depreciation systems. The most generally applicable of these systems is called the *modified accelerated cost recovery* system (MACRS). Under MACRS, when tangible property is placed in service, the cost or other basis of property is recovered over the recovery period specified by the tax rules for the asset. The MACRS has built into it the following two historical depreciation methods:

1. *The straight-line method*—which recovers the cost of an asset, in equal annual installments over its useful life. This method defers a major portion of your depreciation deductions to future years, when you may really need it. For purposes of computing the depreciation allowable under the AMT rules in determining *book income* adjustments and preferences (section 3.12), the straight-line method is called the *alternative depreciation system* (ADS), with only one depreciation period allowed for personal property and one for realty.

2. *The declining-balance method*—which, each year, applies a uniform percentage rate (as much as twice the rate you'd use in a straight-line computation) to the asset's cost, less any depreciation

you have already taken. In effect, you are given extra-large deductions in the early years of the life of an asset, deductions that are more than welcome if your income needs the offset at that time.

A major disadvantage inherent in any accelerated depreciation formula is the tax rule that requires *recapture* of the "excess," or accelerated portion of previously claimed deductions upon an asset's disposition prior to the end of its *useful life* as reflected in the previous deductions. The entire recapture amount is treated as ordinary taxable income upon such disposition, with no opportunity to spread any part of the deemed income forward or backward into other tax years.

The simplest and most advantageous of the depreciation systems is called *first-year expensing,* which permits a 100 percent write-off deduction in the first year of up to $10,000 worth of personal property. The *recapture* tax rules do not apply at all in the case of first-year expensing. However, expensing is not permitted to taxpayers putting more than $210,000 of qualified property into use in one year.

First-year expensing is the only accelerated method of depreciation that has no effect on AMT. Other accelerated methods have two such effects: (1) a direct adjustment to the computation of alternative taxable minimum taxable income (AMTI) and (2) an indirect effect resulting from an adjustment called the *book income* adjustment for corporate AMT. The corporate book-income AMT adjustment attempts to define and tax true economic income (see section 3.12). The result of the different adjustment is a three-track system as follows.

Three-Track System:
System 1: Regular tax system using MACRS depreciation and a 34 percent income tax rate
System 2: AMT system using nonincentive depreciation (usually the *asset depreciation range* (ADR) *system*) and a 20 percent income tax rate
System 3: Book income system using book depreciation and a

10 percent income tax rate (or a 20 percent rate applied to 50 percent of excess book income).

One result of having three systems is that it becomes necessary to keep parallel accounts and books and to analyze transactions on three levels. Depreciation deductions differ under the three systems, the differences being illustrated as follows:

Corporation Z is a calendar-year taxpayer. It puts into service in year 1 a $2,000 special manufacturing dye and a $5,000 metal-cutting lathe. The dye qualifies for three-year class life for regular (MACRS) depreciation, and has an ADR life of four years for AMT calculations and an economic life estimated at eight years for purposes of preparing financial statements. The lathe qualifies for five-year class life for regular (MACRS) depreciation, and has an ADR seven-year life and an estimated fourteen-year economic life. If Corporation Z has income equal to or greater than all tax liability and no other adjustments or preferences affecting AMT, then the various depreciation deductions and AMTI calculations are as shown in Table 3-1 (using the half-year convention).

Depreciation schedules under the three different systems need to be maintained from year to year. Similar parallel recordkeeping is required for net operating losses (NOLs), completed contract method of accounting, and mining development and exploration costs. Running records will be essential for adjusted bases of assets based on deductions allowed under the AMT, minimum tax credit carry-overs, and any AMT foreign tax carry-overs. Taxpayers will have larger depreciation deductions in later years under the AMT (System II) than under the regular tax (System I), a compensation for AMT imposed in earlier years.

For AMTI, the depreciation deduction for property placed in service is computed using the ADR provisions, which generally have longer recovery periods and slower cost recovery than the regular, MACRS provisions. Three-year MACRS property for AMT computation may have a four-year ADR class life and be subject to ADR 150 percent declining balance method instead of the MACRS 200 percent method. Under AMT's ADR system, all realty has a forty-year recovery period, versus twenty-seven and a

Table 3-1. Depreciation deductions for Corporation Z.

Year/ System	Depreciation of Dye	Depreciation of Lathe	Deductions Claimed	AMTI Increase (Decrease)
1/Regular tax	$667	$ 800	$1,467	
/AMT	375	429	804	$663
/Book income	125	143	268	268
2/Regular tax	889	1,280	2,170	
/AMT	609	765	1,374	796
/Book income	250	286	536	419
3/Regular tax	296	768	1,064	
/AMT	406(a)	601	1,007	57
/Book income	250	286	536	236
4/Regular tax	148	461	609	
/AMT	406	490(a)	896	(287)
/Book income	250	286	536	180
5/Regular tax	—	461(a)	461	
/AMT	203	490	693	(232)
/Book income	250	286	536	79
6/Regular tax	—	230	230	
/AMT	—	490	490	(260)
/Book income	250	286	536	(46)
7/Regular tax	—	—	—	
/AMT	—	490	490	(498)
/Book income	250	286	536	(46)
8/Regular tax	—	—	—	
/AMT	—	245	245	(245)
/Book income	250	286	536	(291)
9/Book income	125	286	411	(411)
10–14/Book income	—	286	286	(286)
15/Book income	—	143	143	(143)

(a) In this year, a switch to straight-line depreciation occurs in order to maximize deductions.

half years for residential rental property and thirty-one and a half years for nonresidential property under MACRS.

Use of a rapid recovery method for personal property causes an increase in AMT. However, the AMT depreciation is not computed item by item, so that netting is permitted. Also, there are exceptions in the AMT depreciation rules for sound recordings, film and videotapes depreciated under the income forecast method, property depreciated under the unit-of-production method or other method not expressed in terms of years, and property depreciated using the ADR system.

Since depreciation is computed differently for AMTI than for regular tax purposes, a different gain or loss is realized when a MACRS asset is disposed of prior to full depreciation. For example, the three-year class life asset of Corporation Z (a dye tool) considered in Table 3-1 might be sold on January 1 of year 3 for $2,500, resulting in these different gain calculations:

Regular Tax	*AMT*
Gain = $2,500 less	Gain = $2,500 less
adjusted basis ($444)	adjusted basis ($1,016)
= $2,056	= $1,484

Under System III, for purposes of the corporate book-income adjustment, the ultra-slow depreciation allowance for any tax year is limited to such ratable amount as is necessary to recover the remaining cost or other basis, less salvage value, during the remaining useful life of the property. Neither System II nor System III permits assets to be depreciated below a reasonable salvage value.

3.08   All That's Due

Liabilities are everything the business owes. Like assets, they are categorized on the balance sheet shown in Exhibit 3-2:

Current liabilities (g) are debts due within one year, including short-term notes payable (h), salaries and wages payable, and dividends payable.

Contingent liabilities, those claims that may ripen through litigation, settlement, or the happening of events into full-fledged debts, would also become current liabilities, and might be footnoted here. Subtract current liabilities from current assets, and you will know your total *working capital* (i).

Other liabilities (j) are *fixed liabilities* or *deferred liabilities*. These are long-term private debts (k), including bonds, notes, and mortgages payable, and deferred tax liabilities (l).

3.09   It's All Yours

Shareholders' ownership (m), or *owners' equity* or *net worth*, represents the owners' interest in a business, but not necessarily the distribution of interests upon liquidation. In a proprietorship or partnership, the equity account is merely a composite of capital contributions; retained earnings are viewed as further capital contributions, and withdrawals diminish the capital account. Corporations divide equity into stock ownership—both common (n) and preferred—and surpluses, which may be carved into credit-balance reserve accounts for the future payment of dividends to shareholders and for other prospective liabilities.

3.10   How Are You Doing?

The *income statement* or *statement of profit and loss* (P&L) looks at the dynamic flow of your business. A whole year's activity may be summarized in terms of profit or loss. Exhibit 3-3 offers a bare-bones, but actual, income statement. Note these elements in particular:

▶ *Net sales* (a) is your gross income, less any returns and allowances. In a service business, the label might be *operating income*.

▶ *Selling and administrative expenses* (c) are general operating expenses apart from the cost of goods sold. These include salaries, rent, utilities, advertising costs, depreciation, and all kinds of other deductions that are not directly inventory related.

Exhibit 3-3. Income statement.

WHAT-A-COMPANY
Income Statement
Year Ended December 31, 19x3

(a) Net sales and operating revenues	$630,105
Operating costs:	
(b) Cost of goods sold	421,180
(c) Selling and administrative expenses	140,745
Total operating costs	561,925
(d) Income from operations	68,180
Sundry charges—net	12,880
Income before taxes on income	55,300
Taxes on income	13,825
(e) *Net income for the year*	$ 41,475
Average shares outstanding	11,880
(f) *Earnings per share*	$3.49

▶ *Income from operations* (d) is a pretax profit figure, which may be supplemented by *Extraordinary* or *nonoperating income* and reduced by *extraordinary* or *nonoperating expenses.*

▶ *Net income for the year* (e) is the bottom-line report of your success, which may then be allocated among the owners of your business (f). Net income is carried forward to the balance sheet as a credit to the owners' equity account and as a corresponding debt to fixed or current assets, or a combination of both, depending upon the destination of your profit dollars.

▶ Cost of goods sold (b) is a deduction from net sales, calculated by adding the *inventory*—articles held for sale to customers in the regular course of business (including production costs, if you are a manufacturer)—at the beginning of the accounting period to all purchases made during the period, and then by subtracting the inventory at the close of the period. The lower the ending inventory, the lower the net profit, and the lower your income tax. That's why your identification and valuation of inventories is so closely scrutinized by the IRS.

The first step in computing inventories is counting or guesstimating the actual number of articles available for sale and identifying the articles still on hand—rarely an easy task. Be sure to include all finished goods, work in progress, and raw materials and supplies that have been acquired for sale or that will become part of goods to be sold. Consider any goods to which you have title, even if they are in transit. One of these inventory-identification techniques should help:

▶ *Direct matching.* Each item is individually matched with its true cost or market value. Use direct matching if the sheer size of your inventory won't make it impractical.

▶ *Last in, first out (LIFO).* The items most recently purchased are assumed to be the first items sold. LIFO makes sense in times of inflationary prices because the most recent and highest prices apply for valuation purposes, and the smallest profit and tax result. Those who use LIFO must do so for both financial and tax accounting purposes, and they must value inventories at cost. A switch to LIFO requires IRS approval and fancy accounting reconciliations.

▶ *Dollar-value LIFO.* This takeoff on LIFO may be used for large, homogeneous inventories. Rather than counting units, dollar-value LIFO takes the dollar value of the opening and closing inventories and adjusts to reflect the rise or fall in prices.

▶ *Retail LIFO.* Popular with large retail outlets, retail LIFO is similar to dollar-value LIFO in theory, but is based on retail prices adjusted for markups and markdowns.

▶ *First in, first out (FIFO).* The reverse of LIFO, this method assumes that the first items purchased are the first items sold. FIFO holds profits down in times of falling prices.

Once you have determined the identity and quantity of inventory items, how do you judge their worth? In general, inventories are valued in one of three ways:

1. *Cost.* This is the most common method of valuing inventories. For retail businesses, cost means what you paid plus shipping and handling charges minus discounts. For producers, cost means the total of all raw materials, overhead, labor, and other related expenses.

2. *Cost or market, whichever is lower.* The market value of purchased goods is the current prevailing price; manufacturers are held to the current cost of reproducing goods. This method requires that each item be valued at the lower of cost or market value.

3. *Market.* This method is available only to dealers in securities and some commodities.

3.11 Your Piece of the Pie

The *statement of owners' equity* or *statement of retained earnings* is the third basic piece in your accounting system. Although form and complexity vary dramatically, this report will always show the owners' rights at the beginning and at the end of the subject period, and it will account for the difference. Note these principal calculations in Exhibit 3-4:

▶ *Retained earnings, starting balance (a).* A proprietorship or partnership would show the balance in the owners' equity account on the first day of the period. However captioned, this is the starting point.

Exhibit 3-4. Statement of retained earnings.

WHAT-A-COMPANY
Statement of Retained Earnings
Year Ended December 31, 19X3

(a) Retained earnings, beginning as previously reported	$145,725
(b) Net income for the year	41,475
(c) Dividends	—
(d) Retained earnings, ending	$187,200

► *Net profits and contributions (b)*. Add any net operating profit, earnings from investments, and owners' capital contributions.

► *Losses and withdrawals (c)*. Deduct any net operating loss, casualty loss, distributions to owners as withdrawals or dividends, and retained earnings capitalized as stock.

► *Retained earnings, ending balance (d)*. This is the dollars-and-cents response to the inescapable question, "What have I got?"

3.12 Corporate AMT and Book Income

Many business decisions, especially if a corporate form of organization is involved, require some consideration of *alternative minimum tax* and the *book income tax preference*. You should understand what these terms refer to, and so we'll give you a brief explanation here.

All taxpayers, except S corporations and partnerships that flow their income and expenses through to their owners, are subject to AMT. The AMT is an amount equal to the excess, if any, of "tentative minimum tax" over the regular tax. "Tentative minimum tax" is 20 percent for corporations and 21 percent for other taxpayers, based on AMTI after deducting any AMT foreign tax credit.

AMTI in general is taxable income plus or minus various *adjustments* and plus *tax preferences*, with an *exemption* that, for corporations and married couples filing jointly, is $40,000 less 25 percent of AMTI over $150,000. The provisions for "adjustments" and "preferences" involve substituting special treatment for certain tax items—this substitution is to be done only for the purposes of calculating AMTI. For instance, the substitution to be done in the case of depreciation generally requires depreciation adjustments as follows:

1. The AMTI deductions for most depreciable real property and property depreciated under the straight-line method for regular tax purposes is computed under the ADS System (see section 3.07).

2. The AMTI deductions for all other property are computed using the 150 percent declining balance method (switching to straight-line in the year necessary to maximize the allowance).

3. The amounts determined in items 1 and 2 are subtracted from the corresponding MACRS calculations for the same properties to derive the AMTI adjustments.

For certain fairly rare kinds of property, there may be depreciation preferences to be added to AMTI in addition to making the adjustments required for ordinary items.

While often referred to as a tax preference, the substitution involved in calculating corporate *book income* is really an adjustment. That adjustment is equal to one-half of the amount, if any, by which a corporation's *adjusted net book income* exceeds AMTI (as determined without the book income adjustment and before any AMT net operating loss is deducted). The term "adjusted net book income" refers to the net income or loss shown on the corporation's *applicable financial statement* for the respective tax year; "applicable financial statement" means the first listed, and applicable, document from a list of documents as follows: (1) the statement that a corporation files for regulatory or credit purposes, (2) a shareholder report, or (3) other report of earnings prepared for nontax purposes.

3.13   What Does It All Mean?

Successful business managers universally agree that the better informed their decision making is, the more effective it is apt to be. Your intelligent and thoughtful interpretation of financial data should pay off handsomely.

1. *See how you fared this year as compared with last year;* Comparisons will guide you. You'll see your growth in its logical context. See how one profit center scored against another; expose your weaknesses and correct or eliminate them. See how you did in comparison with the competition; learn from their mistakes and their victories.

2. *Rely on ratio analysis.* Comparing one accounting element with another can reveal nearly everything about the real condition of a business. Check these key ratios in your enterprise:

▶ *Working capital.* The ratio of current assets to liabilities will tell you how easily you meet your immediate obligations. To be conservative, subtract inventories from current assets in assessing your bill-paying ability.

▶ *Net income to net worth.* This is the percentage of return on invested capital, especially important to you as an investor.

▶ *Net profit to net sales.* This is a test of profitability. If you fall short of the competition, insist on a cost accounting analysis to learn why.

3. *Treat financial statements as educational building blocks.* Graduate to specialized reports that will offer a closer look at acute problems, and focus on data particularly interesting or important to shareholders or potential investors. Consider monthly sales analyses, analyses of production costs, and any other reports that will prove useful to you as you direct the growth of your business and attract support in that effort.

4. *Use what you learn.* Don't slap backs with shining financial reports; seek out danger signs. Watch for top-heavy fixed assets, uncontrolled liabilities, and excessive inventories—and act. Possibly no one else will.

4 Developing Something Special

Intellectual products alone are imperishable.

—William Osler

4.01 Protecting Intellectual Property

Good ideas are a vital force in the growth of any successful business. Understandably, you will want to preserve the unique business ideas you create. Yet pure thought cannot be owned by anyone—not by you and not by your competition. The law will protect a property right in ideas only when those ideas have been reduced to a recognizable form or expression. Hence are the most common ways to establish such intellectual property:

▶ *Patent*—the exclusive right to use, manufacture, and sell the concrete expression of a novel and useful idea or design. Governed by federal law, patents are granted for limited time periods prescribed by statute.
▶ *Trade secret*—business know-how and, in fact, any confidential information you maintain for the good of your business. Trade secrets are protected by common-law concepts embodied in state laws. These laws prohibit others from wrongfully breaching such secrecy, either through the commission of a tort or the violation of an express or implied contract.
▶ *Copyright*—a common-law, or statutory, right that protects literary and artistic property from unauthorized reproduction or performance.
▶ *Trademark*—a word, name, symbol, or device used to distin-

62

guish and identify your product by indicating its origin that may be registered under state and federal laws. A trademark serves to guarantee a product's quality and indeed creates and sustains a demand for the product.

▶ *Contract*—between the creator and the user of intellectual property to fix and ensure its value.

4.02 Patents

Prerequisites

Although a patent will exclude others from using, manufacturing, and selling your product without your authority, it will not safeguard your invention's secrecy, nor will it prevent other inventors from improving on your idea and patenting their own "new" products. Even your rights to exclusivity will expire in seventeen years, leaving your product idea vulnerable to expropriation. Nonetheless, a patent is probably the best protection available to an inventor. See if you meet the following three requirements:

1. *You must be the original inventor.* Obviously, you may not receive a patent on someone else's brainstorm. And even if the idea is your own, it may lose its patentability after others gain access to it, perhaps through descriptions in print or through public use.

2. *Your idea must be novel, nonobvious, and concrete in form.* Only a utilitarian application of an idea can be patented, not the naked idea itself. So scientific principles like Einstein's theory of relativity just don't qualify. Neither do concepts or combinations of concepts that are old hat, or solutions that might occur to just anyone. Yet an idea need not be mysterious to be judged nonobvious: A safety pin, for instance, seems like a very obvious answer to an age-old need, but only after you've seen one.

3. *Your idea must fall into one of the three patentable categories:* (a) *Utility inventions* (any new and useful process, machine, manufacture, composition of matter, or new and useful improvement of one of the foregoing—which may include a genetically new animal

but not a software program); (b) *ornamental designs* (any design that is both useful and ornamental, such as a new auto bumper or football helmet); or (c) *asexually reproduced plants* other than tuber-propagated plants.

Procedures

Having satisfied yourself that your idea appears patentable, bring in an attorney. The Patent and Trademark Office requires even lawyers to get a special license. In fact, most patent practitioners have both legal and engineering training. A competent specialist will guide you through the incredibly tedious patent process.

First, you'll need to reduce your invention to written form, in precise verbal and pictorial detail. To prove you were the first inventor of the product you define, you'll need to establish the date of your invention. All this material will be sent to the Patent and Trademark Office as a *disclosure document,* where it will be held confidentially for two years while you seek to secure your patent. This procedure will help establish your invention date.

The next step is a private patent search conducted by special researchers in Washington, D.C., who are trained in the issues of patentability. After concluding that your invention is patentable, your attorney will file an application on your behalf, along with the necessary fee.

Finally, the Patent and Trademark Office will issue its *office action,* accepting, objecting to, or rejecting your application. Should it be objected to or rejected, you will have from three to six months to clarify or improve your filing. If your application is rejected twice on the same ground, administrative and judicial appeals will be your recourse.

Peculiarities

Once you have obtained your *notice of allowance* and, ultimately, your patent, you'll enjoy all the exclusive rights it confers. Protect those rights by respecting the laws that will now govern your invention:

1. Don't forget to mark your product or its package with the word "patented" (or "pat.") and the patent number. Patent marking

constitutes legal notice to a would-be infringer, notice that will support a suit for damages. But be aware that markings such as "Patent pending" or "Patent applied for" serve only to inform the public of your intent and are frequently adopted for dubious promotional purposes. They are subject to fines if not true, and otherwise have no legal effect because patent rights commence only with the patent's issuance and are never retroactive.

2. Watch out for antitrust problems. Using, licensing, or assigning a patent in any way that unlawfully restrains trade, fixes prices, or reduces competition may be grounds for the termination of your patent rights (see section 5.01).

3. At all times, remember that your rights are controlled by the federal government, so don't treat the patent as your absolute property. Should you sell your patent, for instance, the assignment must be recorded in the Patent and Trademark Office within three months, or your purchaser will not succeed to your rights.

4.03 You've Got a Secret

The patent laws offer only a limited solution to your big need for intellectual property protection. Most business ideas are simply not patentable. Those that are may not be ripe for the public disclosure our patent laws require. And, sometimes most important, patents can be very costly.

Often a better answer is reliance on various state trade secret laws, which protect the owners of business secrets by guaranteeing their right to privacy and by guarding against betrayals of confidence by associates and employees. Anyone is free to use your secret, but only after discovering it fairly or developing it independently. Unlike a patented product or idea whose substance is reserved to its creator after public disclosure, a trade secret derives its very vitality from the fact that it is not disclosed. The legal protection afforded trade secrets thus hinges on your ability to show that your idea is worth protecting and that you intend to preserve its secrecy. Keep these three points in mind:

1. Protect only those secrets worth protecting. If outsiders already know what you know, or if they can gain your knowledge with little effort, protective measures are futile.

2. Limit access to genuinely valuable information—customer lists, plans, processes, formulas, or any ideas that set you apart from your competition. Only those employees who need to know secrets should be able to learn them, and they should be required to respect the confidentiality of your trade secrets.

3. Demand that all personnel sign *restrictive covenants*, which might be incorporated into their employment contracts. Such covenants would acknowledge that you have developed and own information that is to be treated confidentially and that this information may be divulged to the employees only if they agree to keep it secret and to return any confidential documents in their possession when their employment is concluded.

4.04   Copyrighting Your Writing and More

Copyrights offer the best protection for literary and artistic intellectual property, including computer software programs. Unlike patents and trade secrets, a copyright relates to the exact form of expression, not the substantive idea it represents. For this reason, the copyright becomes valuable only when the form itself is worth preserving, as in the case of poetry, music, art, or advertising copy. No protection is available for ideas, systems, concepts, or principles.

The Federal Copyright Act now preempts most common-law copyrights for any work fixed in a tangible medium of expression. The Copyright Law generally gives the owner of the copyright the exclusive right to do and to authorize others to do the following:

► *To reproduce* the copyrighted work in copies or phonorecords
► *To prepare derivative works* based upon the copyrighted work
► *To distribute copies or phonorecords* of the copyrighted work to

the public by sale or other transfer of ownership, or by rental, lease, or lending

▶ *To perform the copyrighted work publicly*, in the case of literary, musical, dramatic, and choreographic works, pantomimes, and motion pictures and other audiovisual works

▶ *To display the copyrighted work publicly*, in the case of literary, musical, dramatic, and choreographic works, pantomimes, and pictorial, graphic, or sculptural works, including the individual images of a motion picture or other audiovisual work

Today, composers, software program designers, artists, writers, other professionals who create copy, and their publishers should enlist the aid of attorneys in obtaining and protecting their copyrights. This is because a copyright infringement suit cannot be brought unless the work has been registered in the Copyright Office in the Library of Congress.

Prior registration thus becomes a condition to any infringement action for statutory damages and attorney fees. The copyright owner's rights are not affirmatively granted by any government agency but are secured by the creator who complies with the copyright laws. Here are the requirements:

1. The material must be subject to copyright. Ideas, systems, and methods do not qualify; only forms of expression can be protected. Other ineligibles are slogans, titles, symbols, names, works that merely record information (such as diaries and address books), and works that contain only universally known information (including calendars and rulers).

2. The material must be original. It can be of any one of different categories such as the following:

▶ Literary works
▶ Musical works, including any accompanying words
▶ Dramatic works, including any accompanying music
▶ Pantomimes and choreographic works
▶ Pictorial, graphic, and sculptural works
▶ Motion pictures and other audiovisual works
▶ Sound recordings

The list is illustrative and very broad—computer software programs are registrable as "literary works," and architectural blueprints are registrable as "pictorial, graphic, and sculptural works."

3. The material must be fixed in a tangible medium of expression (usually a copy or phonographic record).

4. Copies of the material must be produced with a *copyright notice* in the prescribed position. Generally, the notice will consist of the word "copyright," the abbreviation "copr.," or the universally recognized symbol ©; the copyright owner's name; and the year of publication—

© Creative Prodigy 19x3

5. Your claim should be registered in the Copyright Office. The application for registration, which varies with the class or work, must be accompanied by two copies of the best edition of the work as published (or one copy if it is to remain unpublished) and a registration fee. For original registrations, one of the following forms is required:

Form TX: For published and unpublished nondramatic literary works

Form SE: For serials, works issued or intended to be issued in successive parts bearing numerical or chronological designations and intended to be continued indefinitely (periodicals, newspapers, magazines, newsletters, annuals, journals)

Form PA: For published and unpublished works of the performing arts (musical and dramatic works, pantomimes and choreographic works, motion pictures, and other audiovisual works)

Form VA: For published and unpublished works of the visual arts (pictorial, graphic, and sculptural works)

Form SR: For published and unpublished sound recordings

The application process is a simple one, but any questions about the specifics will be answered if you contact the Register of Copyrights, Library of Congress, Washington, D.C. 20559.

Copyrights and Wrongs

Over forty countries are signatories to an international copy-right convention/treaty called the Berne Union, although the United States was not among them at the time this book was written. By arranging a first publication date simultaneously in this country and in a Berne Union member country, it is possible to gain legal copyright protection both here and in all the signatory countries. Details as to the foreign country members and laws are available from The Secretariat, International Bureau of the World Intellectual Property Organization (WIPO), 32, Chemin des Columbettes, 1211 Geneva 20 Switzerland.

The proper registration of your copyright in the United States will entitle you to protection, but your rights will be limited. Be aware that:

1. *The burden of proving an unauthorized use or infringement rests with you.* You must prove that the infringer had access to your work and actually used it.

2. *Some uses of your copyrighted work are permitted, even in the absence of your authority.* For example, the private and incidental use of your material, or a reasonable quotation in a review or bio-graphical work, is a permissible *fair use.* The general enjoyment and diffusion of knowledge—as opposed to its commercial exploi-tation—is encouraged by the courts. Recording rights in musical works are restricted by *compulsory license,* which automatically au-thorizes recordings of a composition (upon the payment of royalties) as soon as the composer OKs the initial recording of the work.

3. *A copyright will neither protect the content of your work nor its exclusivity.* Ideas are not copyrightable. The Copyright Office makes no search of its records to see if a similar or even identical filing has been made by someone else.

4.05 Trading With Trademarks

The legal protection of a *trademark* stems from the laws against "unfair competition" in business and not from any individual ownership rights. That being the case, the registration of a trademark alone will not qualify it for protection; only its commercial use will ensure your trademark rights.

As with any commercially valuable asset, you should strive to develop trademarks that will enhance your business image. After all, the function of a trademark is to identify a product and to create and maintain a demand for it. You and your attorney should seek to enhance your goodwill in the selection of trademarks and avoid the following:

1. *Initials and third-party names.* The names or signature of any living person cannot be used without his consent. Several states prohibit unauthorized commercial use of a deceased person's name if descendants of such decedent reside in those states.

2. *Federal or state symbols and the name or likeness of a deceased U.S. president whose widow is still alive.*

3. A *descriptive name or symbol.* Opt for one that's suggestive. Better yet, choose one that's wholly original. Any mark that's deceptively similar to an existing mark is an invitation to a lawsuit. For this reason and others, your lawyer may wisely suggest a trademark search.

4. *Any mark that is immoral, deceptive, scandalous, or sacrilegious in nature.*

Why Federal Trademarks Are Better Than State

The Lanham Act permits federal registration of any trademark used in interstate commerce. Many local businesses, especially service businesses, are limited to protection under state law, since they do not qualify under the Act. Those that do qualify are well advised to follow through with federal registration. Here's why:

1. Federal trademark laws have been liberally expanded to include *service marks* (used to identify services rather than goods), *certification marks* (third-party marks such as union-made labels used to certify origin, materials, manufacturing processes, or overall quality), and *collective marks* (service or trademarks used by cooperatives or organizations to signify membership).

2. Federal registration gives nationwide protection in blocking the later registration of deceptively similar marks by others.

3. Federal registration prevents the importation of any goods bearing a deceptively similar mark.

4. Federal registration grants the registrant the broader and often better protection the federal courts offer.

Registering Your Mark

For the reasons just listed, if your business qualifies as interstate commerce, you will certainly want to register your marks with the U.S. Commissioner of Patents and Trademarks. Consider making application for the *Principal Register* or the *Supplemental Register.*

The *Principal Register* is limited to "technical marks," those that are coined, arbitrary, fanciful, or suggestive. Excluded are those based on descriptive names and surnames, unless they have been in commercial use for five years or more and have clearly become identified with your product or service. Only the *Principal Register* issues notice to the world, rejecting deceptively similar marks on imports. Registration is for twenty years, renewable for additional twenty-year periods indefinitely.

The *Supplemental Register* is for marks that have been used for a year or more and that are capable of distinguishing goods but do not qualify for the *Principal Register.* The *Supplemental Register's* standards are broader, allowing any symbol, label, package, configuration of goods, word, slogan, phrase, surname, geographical name, numeral, or device. Although notice of ownership is not construed from supplemental registration, it does establish the right to sue in U.S. courts. Registration is good for twenty years and cannot be renewed, except to support a foreign registration.

Your application for registration can be filed only after your trademark is used in interstate commerce. Many times, this means preparing a label bearing the mark, affixing it to the product, and consummating a token sale across state lines. The mark is then officially in interstate use, and the application for registration can be filed. In brief, these are the filing requirements:

1. You must submit a written application. Exhibit 4-1 shows various classes of goods and services. Find yours and enter it on the application blank, which you can obtain (along with instructions) from a low-cost pamphlet entitled *Basic Facts About Trademarks,* prepared by the Patent and Trademark Office of the U.S. Commerce Department (available from the Superintendent of Documents, U.S. Government Printing Office, Washington, D.C. 20402).

2. Your application must be accompanied by a drawing of the mark, in black ink on white paper, with a specified heading near the top. Various requirements apply to the size of the drawing and the use of certain linings to indicate colors.

3. With your application, you will also need to submit five specimens of the mark. These should be duplicates of actual labels, tags, or containers, unless specimens are impractical, in which event photos can be substituted.

4. A registration fee will be required.

Once your application is approved, either on initial examination or subsequent reexamination or after an appeal to the Trademark Trial and Appeal Board, the *Official Gazette* will publish your mark. Anyone who believes your mark constitutes an infringement of an existing mark will have thirty days to file an opposition or application for cancellation of the mark. Oppositions, which may be filed before a certificate of registration is issued, and cancellation petitions, which can be filed after such issuance, are both heard by the Trial and Appeal Board.

Your Continuing Trademark Obligations

If no protests are lodged, or if all protests are resolved in your favor, you will ultimately receive a *certificate of registration,* entitling your goods to carry the legend "Registered in U.S. Patent and Trademarks Office" or "Reg. U.S. Pat. & Tm. Off." or the familiar symbol ®. It will then become your ongoing obligation to preserve that privilege in all the following ways:

Exhibit 4-1. Trademark and servicemark classifications (international schedule of classes of goods and services).

Goods

1 Chemicals, products used in industry, science, photography, agriculture, horticulture, forestry; artificial and synthetic resins; plastics in the form of powders, liquids, or pastes, for industrial use; manures (natural and artificial); fire extinguishing compositions; tempering substances and chemical preparations for soldering; chemical substances for preserving foodstuffs; tanning substances; adhesive substances used in industry.

2 Paints, varnishes, lacquers; preservatives against rust and against deterioration of wood; coloring matters, dyestuffs, mordants; natural resins; metals in foil and powder form for painters and decorators.

3 Bleaching preparations and other substances for laundry use; cleaning, polishing, scouring and abrasive preparations; soaps; perfumery, essential oils, cosmetics, hair lotions; dentifrices.

4 Industrial oils and greases (other than oils and fats and essential oils); lubricants; dust laying and absorbing compositions; fuels (including moror spirit) and illuminants; candles, tapers, night lights and wicks.

5 Pharmaceutical, veterinary, and sanitary substances; infants; and invalids' foods; plasters, material for bandaging; material for stopping teeth, dental wax, disinfectants; preparations for killing weeds and destroying vermin.

6 Unwrought and partly wrought common metals and their alloys; anchors, anvils, bells, rolled and cast building materials; rails and other metallic materials for railway tracks; chains (except driving chains for vehicles); cables and wires (nonelectric); locksmiths' work; metallic pipes and tubes; safes and cash boxes; steel balls; horseshoes; nails and screws; other goods in nonprecious metal not included in other classes; ores.

7 Machines and machine tools; motors (except for land vehicles); machine couplings and belting (except for land vehicles); large size agricultural implements; incubators.

8 Hand tools and instruments; cutlery, forks, and spoons; side arms.

9 Scientific, nautical, surveying, and electrical apparatus and instruments (including wireless), photographic, cinematographic, optical, weighing, measuring, signalling, checking (supervision), life-saving and teaching apparatus and instruments; coin or counterfreed apparatus; talking machines; cash registers; calculating machines; fire extinguishing apparatus.

10 Surgical, medical, dental, and veterinary instruments and apparatus (including artificial limbs, eyes, and teeth).

11 Installations for lighting, heating, steam generating, cooking, refrigerating, drying, ventilating, water supply, and sanitary purposes.

12 Vehicles; apparatus for locomotion by land, air, or water.

13 Firearms; ammunition and projectiles; explosive substances; fireworks.

(continued)

Exhibit 4-1. *Continued*

14 Precious metals and their alloys and goods in precious metals or coated therewith (except cutlery, forks, and spoons); jewelry, precious stones, horological, and other chronometric instruments.

15 Musical instruments (other than talking machines and wireless apparatus).

16 Paper and paper articles, cardboard and cardboard articles; printed matter, newspaper and periodicals, books; bookbinding material; photographs; stationery, adhesive materials (stationery); artists' materials; paint brushes; typewriters and office requisites (other than furniture); instructional and teaching material (other than apparatus); playing cards; printers' type and clichés (stereotype).

17. Gutta percha, india rubber, balata and substitutes, articles made from these substances and not included in other classes; plastics in the form of sheets, blocks, and rods, being for use in manufacture; materials for packing, stopping, or insulating; asbestos, mica and their products; hose pipes (nonmetallic).

18 Leather and imitations of leather, and articles made from these materials and not included in other classes; skins, hides; trucks, and travelling bags; umbrellas, parasols, and walking sticks; whips, harness, and saddlery.

19 Building materials, natural and artificial stone, cement, lime, mortar, plaster, and gravel; pipes of earthenware or cement; roadmaking materials; asphalt, pitch, and bitumen; portable buildings; stone monuments; chimney pots.

20 Furniture, mirrors, picture frames; articles (not included in other classes) of wood, cork, reeds, cane, wicker, horn, bone, ivory, whalebone, shell, amber, mother-of-pearl, meerschaum, celluloid, substitutes for all these materials, or plastics.

21 Small domestic utensils and containers (not of precious metals or coated therewith); combs and sponges; brushes (other than paint brushes); brushmaking materials; instruments and material for cleaning purposes, steel wool; unworked or semi-worked glass (excluding glass used in building); glassware, porcelain, and earthenware not included in other classes.

22 Ropes; string, nets, tents, awnings; tarpaulins, sails, sacks; padding and stuffing materials (hair, kapok, feathers, seaweed, etc.); raw fibrous textile materials.

23 Yarns; threads.

24 Tissues (piece goods); bed and table covers; textile articles not included in other classes.

25 Clothing, including boots, shoes, and slippers.

26 Lace and embroidery, ribands and braid; buttons, press buttons, hooks and eyes, pins and needles; artificial flowers.

27 Carpets, rugs, mats and matting; linoleums and other materials for covering existing floors; wall hangings (nontextile).

Exhibit 4-1. *Continued*

28 Games and playthings; gymnastic and sporting articles (except clothing); ornaments and decorations for Christmas trees.

29 Meats, fish, poultry, and game; meat extracts; preserved, dried, and cooked fruits and vegetables; jellies, jams; eggs, milk, and other dairy products; edible oils and fats; preserves, pickles.

30 Coffee, tea, cocoa, sugar, rice, tapioca, soap; coffee substitutes; flour and preparations made from cereals; bread, biscuits, cakes, pastry and confectionary, ices; hone, treacle; yeast, baking powder; salt, mustard, pepper, vinegar, sauces, spices; ice.

31 Agricultural, horticultural, and forestry products and grains not included in other classes; live plants and flowers; foodstuffs for animals, malt.

32 Beer, ale, and porter; mineral and aerated waters and other nonalcoholic drinks; syrups and other preparations for making beverages.

33 Wines, spirits, and liqueurs.

34 Tobacco, raw or manufactured; smokers' articles; matches.

Services

35 Advertising and business.
36 Insurance and financial.
37 Construction and repair.
38 Communication.
39 Transportation and storage.
40 Material treatment.
41 Education and entertainment.
42 Miscellaneous.

Source: U.S. Department of Commerce/Patent and Trademark Office. (Form PTO-1478 FB (ref. 4/87))

1. *Use your trademark properly.* Display the mark (exactly as registered) distinctly and conspicuously to identify your goods. Use it consistently to modify the generic name, with no words inserted between any words that are actual parts of the trademark. If it's a word, always capitalize it and use it as an adjective, never as a noun or verb. "Thermos" and "cellophane" were lost as trademarks because their owners failed to distinguish them as brands rather than generic terms. And by all means, use the mark continually; disuse can be labeled an abandonment of the mark and of your rights to it.

2. *Protect your mark.* Be on the lookout for any potential and actual infringements, and report them. Check the *Official Gazette* each week (or have your lawyer do it), and file a timely protest against any similar mark in a pending application.

3. *File the affidavits you need.* An *Affidavit* or *Declaration of Use* must be filed with the Patent and Trademark Office during the sixth year after registration. This document must include the number and date of your certificate of registration and an affirmation that the mark—a sample of which should be attached—is still in use. Failure to comply will result in cancellation of your registration.

Under certain circumstances, you can also file an *Affidavit* or *Declaration of Incontestability.* This filing firmly establishes your rights in your mark and exempts it from proceedings before the Trial and Appeal Board. An affidavit may be submitted only after the mark has been registered and continuously used for five years, and only if you have received no adverse decision concerning your right to use the mark and there is no pending proceeding on that point.

Both the *Affidavit* or *Declaration of Use* and the *Affidavit* or *Declaration of Incontestability* may be combined into a single document setting forth the number and date of your certificate of registration and the affirmations: (a) that the mark—a sample of which should be attached—is still in use, (b) that there has been no final decision adverse to your claim of ownership of the mark, or to your right to register it or keep it on the register, and (c) that there is no proceeding involving such rights pending and not disposed of either in the Patent and Trademark Office or in the courts.

4. *Renew your rights.* Marks on the *Principal Register* must be renewed during the last half of the twentieth year. The renewal application includes roughly the same information as the Affidavit (or Declaration) of Use and should be accompanied by the statutory fee.

5. *Register any change in ownership.* If the mark is sold, even as part of the business goodwill, this change calls for registration. The new owner will succeed to the unexpired portion of the original term of registration.

4.06   Contracting With the Creative

In addition to the intellectual property you develop, you will no doubt want to use and protect the applied ideas of employees, independent consulting contractors, and even outsiders with no relationship to the enterprise. Here are a few ways your business can best deal with the creative work done for you by other people:

▶ *Intellectual property created by an employee* will be owned by him, unless his employment agreement provides otherwise. Nevertheless, you will gain a *shop right* to use any property developed at work with employer materials, and you can establish even clearer rights by having your employees contractually assign to you any inventions they may create in the course of employment.

▶ *Intellectual property created by a consultant* should become yours through a carefully drafted agreement, specifically assigning to you all the ideas and inventions developed in the course of his service, and binding him to keep his discoveries secret from the outside world. At the same time, he can contract not to divulge confidential information learned while rendering his services.

▶ *Intellectual property created by an outsider* can impose serious legal liabilities on the business that uses it without having received a written release like this one:

[*date*]

Through the attached descriptions and sketches, I, Genuine Genius, hereby voluntarily disclose to Yourgood Company my design for the "Brand-New Widget." This disclosure was unsolicited by Yourgood Company, which is not obligated to adopt my submission in any way. The company may retain any material I submit, and it may make copies of such material to preserve the record. No confidential relationship is created by this disclosure or by any prior or subsequent disclosure. All my rights and Yourgood Company's obligations are expressly limited to those provided by the United States Patent Statutes, yet Yourgood Company does not hereby obtain a license under any patent rights by this submission.

[*Signature*]

(*text continues on page 81*)

Exhibit 4-2. Confidentiality and nonuse agreement.

DATE: ————————————, 19———

PARTIES: Inventor Company, Inc.
               1 You—Name—It Street
               Anycity, Anystate 00000 ("Inventor-Co")

               Exploiter Company, Inc.
               2 You—Name—It Street
               Anycity, Anystate 00000 ("Exploiter-Co")

RECITALS:

    1. Inventor-Co has developed technical blue-prints, designs, styles, drawings, and concept pictures (the "Data") for widgets.

    2. The parties wish to discuss the Data with a view toward the possibility of Exploiter-Co's using same in products to be sold in the United States of America and abroad.

    3. The parties wish at this time to establish confidentiality and nonuse terms governing their discussions, recognizing that before Exploiter-Co has the right to use any of the Data, a further license agreement will be required between the parties in order to set forth applicable terms.

AGREEMENTS:

In consideration of the covenants, conditions, and agreements set forth below, the parties hereby agree as follows:

1. Treatment of Data

The Data for widgets is both proprietary and confidential, and Exploiter-Co agrees to treat the Data as being trade secrets owned and belonging to Inventor-Co. No Data shall be photocopied or copied in any manner by

Exhibit 4-2. *Continued*

Exploiter-Co's personnel without specific written permission from Inventor-Co. Nothing contained herein or
any material or information furnished pursuant to this
Agreement shall constitute a warranty or inducement by
either party to the other with respect to the infringement of patent, copyright, or other rights of third
parties.

2. Term of Agreement

The term of this Agreement shall be for 90 days from
the date first set forth above.

3. Duration of Confidentiality and Nonuse

Exploiter-Co agrees to treat the Data as confidential
for a period of ten years from the date of disclosure,
subject to any license agreement which the parties may
hereafter enter into. During such period, Exploiter-Co
agrees not to use the Data and to treat the Data in the
same manner as it treats its own proprietary or confidential information, limiting dissemination to those of
its personnel having a "need to know." Such restrictions are not applicable to information previously
known to Exploiter-Co, rightfully acquired from third
parties or publicly disclosed by Inventor-Co. The provisions of this paragraph shall survive the expiration
of the term of this Agreement.

4. Representations

Exploiter-Co represents that it has appropriate understandings with its employees and others whose services
it may use sufficient to enable it to comply with the
terms of this Agreement.

5. License Agreement Not Obligatory

Exploiter-Co shall not be considered obligated in any
way to enter into a subsequent license agreement providing for the exploitation or use of the Data.

(continued)

Exhibit 4-2. *Continued*

6. Return of Data

All materials made available by Inventor–Co to Exploiter–Co under this Agreement, and all copies of such materials made by Exploiter–Co, shall be transmitted by Exploiter–Co to Inventor–Co within 30 days following the end of the term of this Agreement.

7. No Assignment

Neither party shall have a right to assign or delegate all or any part of this Agreement without the prior written consent of the other. Any attempted assignment or delegation made without such consent shall be deemed a substantial breach of this Agreement.

8. Entire Agreement and Nonwaiver

This Agreement contains the entire understanding of the parties, and there are no other agreements between them. Any modification or waiver of any provision of this Agreement must be in writing duly signed on behalf of both parties.

9. Governing Law

This Agreement shall in all respects be governed by the laws of the State of _____. In the event any provision hereof shall be invalid, the other provisions shall remain in full force and effect.

IN WITNESS WHEREOF, the parties have caused this Agreement to be executed on the date first set forth above.

INVENTOR COMPANY, INC.   EXPLOITER COMPANY, INC.

By _____   By _____
        its President   its President

▶ The other side of the creative coin is the situation where your business has the ownership rights in an invention but is not in a position to exploit it. Then, in order to secure a license agreement with a company that can exploit the invention, you may need a preliminary contract under which you can disclose your idea and specifications subject to assurances by the other party that it will neither use nor divulge the invention. If you find yourself in this situation, you should ask your attorney to draw up the form of preliminary contract—you may wish to consider the form provided in Exhibit 4-2.

4.07   Growing Defensively

The legal safeguards afforded intellectual property are indispensable as the fledgling business, or even the mature one, seeks to cope with well-entrenched rivals for the sales dollar. Be vigilant, and periodically review all the ideas and applications that are important to you as well as all those likely to become important to you in the future. Then work with your lawyer in fortifying your creative line of defense against your most vigorous competitors.

5 Selling Your Wares

Set thy person forth to sell.

—Shakespeare

5.01 The Antitrust Philosophy

The American economic system is one of free enterprise, and businesses are encouraged to compete freely and to contract independently. Nonetheless, your relationships with both competitors and customers are governed by a battery of federal and state antitrust laws, enacted to regulate the marketing and distribution of goods and services. For the most part, federal antitrust laws are enforced by the Federal Trade Commission (FTC) and the Department of Justice. Although the laws themselves are complex, their basic purposes are easily understood.

▶ The *Sherman Antitrust Act* seeks to ensure the survival of a competitive, capitalist economy. The Act bars unreasonable restraints that would threaten open competition and thereby tend to create monopolies. Businesses are specifically prohibited from engaging in activities that would unduly restrain others from competing freely—boycotts, price fixing, tying agreements (section 1.10), and now even fair trading.

▶ The *Clayton Act*, amended by the *Robinson-Patman Act* and the *Cellar–Kefauver Act*, guarantees the right of the small business to compete. The Act prohibits discrimination by reason of size or

82

economic power, and outlaws tactics such as unjust price discrimination, total requirements contracts, and the monopolistic acquisition of competitors.

▶ The *Federal Trade Commission Act* defends the public's right to choose among competing goods and services on the basis of their true merit.

Thus, the antitrust laws regulate you, but they regulate your competitors too. The result is a competitive climate in which the small business can exist and thrive. Your growth must be deliberate, but always sensitive to the rights of both your competitors and the public. So—

You may:	But you may not:
Freely choose your customers and suppliers.	Refuse to deal unless your customers or suppliers meet illegal tying, price-fixing, or territory-carving demands.
Enter into reasonable resale or distributorship agreements.	Go beyond what is reasonable to ensure that you can survive and compete. So avoid unduly restrictive agreements, especially with businesses smaller than yours.
Sell the same product under different brands at different prices, offer different qualities of goods at different prices, and sell the same goods at different prices to different classes of customers.	Use pricing to discriminate or compete unfairly (1) by offering the same goods to the same class of customers at different prices (or with other benefits offered to one and not the other) or (2) by coercing suppliers into giving you preferential price treatment or other inducements.

Use any fair means to outdo your competition.	Use predatory tactics, such as bribing your competitors' employees or disparaging their goods and services, excluding them from a market through restrictive contracts, or initiating price wars in order to drive them out of business.
Be friendly with the competition and join them in trade associations and industrywide service organizations.	Cooperate with the competition to limit prices or product, to divide markets, or to initiate boycotts or blacklists.

The antitrust aspects of markets are so detailed and pervasive that we can only hope to convey their flavor here. Antimonopoly provisions of the antitrust laws are explored more fully in section 12.07.

5.02 Advertising and Regulations on Express Warranties

Just as the methods of marketing your goods and services will be regulated from beginning to end, the way your wares are portrayed to the public will also be closely scrutinized by officials at every level of government. Although countless federal acts specifically affect advertising—among them the Magnuson-Moss Consumer Warranty Act, the Communications Act, the Federal Food, Drug and Cosmetics Act, the Consumer Credit Protection Act, the Consumer Products Safety Act, the Trademarks Act, and the Copyright Act—it is the Federal Trade Commission Act that probably has the most powerful impact on business in general. The FTC's power to prevent unfair competition and deceptive practices in or affecting interstate commerce gives it considerable control over advertising content. The FTC's mandate is to monitor radio and television broadcasts of commercial messages, to review ads in print media, and to hear consumer and business complaints, all with a view toward eradicating injury through advertising.

The public's right to truth and accountability has caused the FTC to promulgate rules and regulations covering not only how a product is advertised and sold, but also how it performs after the consumer takes it home. The following are a few basic principles that govern interpretation of "unfair and deceptive practices" and that should be considered in the formulation of your advertising program:

▶ *An advertisement must not tend to mislead or deceive either by picture or word.* Whether your ad actually does mislead or deceive is not the issue. Exaggeration is now held to very strict limits and is acceptable only when it is clearly a statement of opinion—such as "the most beautiful" or "the best tasting"—and not a representation of fact.

▶ *Foreknowledge or intent to deceive on the part of the advertiser is not necessary to prove that an advertisement violates FTC standards.*

▶ *The contents of an ad will be judged in light of the impression it makes on the public.* Recent decisions look at advertisements as the average consumer, one who is credulous and gullible, might. Worse still, advertising to a particular market—the very young or the uneducated, for instance—is examined in light of that specific audience's lesser capacity to understand it.

▶ *The advertiser is held to his express and implied warranties.* So, to the extent that you can, you will want to limit your commitments by means of a *disclaimer.*

The Magnuson–Moss Consumer Warranty Act does not require you to give any warranty to customers. However, if you do provide a warranty, it must have a prominent heading such as "Full Warranty" or "Limited Warranty." The FTC's regulations and guidelines for a full warranty are much more stringent than those applicable to a limited warranty. In general, all *express warranties* in connection with the sale of products require conspicuous and understandable language covering the following:

▶ The identity of the party or parties to whom the warranty is extended.

▶ Whether the warranty is limited to the original consumer purchaser or is otherwise limited to persons other than every consumer owner during the term of the warranty.

▶ A description of the products, parts, characteristics, components, or properties covered by or excluded from the warranty.

▶ What the warrantor will do with respect to a defect, malfunction, or failure.

▶ The time period or other measurement of the warranty's duration.

▶ The procedure that the consumer should follow in order to obtain performance of the warranty.

▶ Information about the availability of any informal dispute settlement mechanism elected by the warrantor.

▶ Any exclusions of or limitations on relief such as incidental or consequential damages, accompanied by this statement:

Some states do not allow the exclusion or limitation of incidental or consequential damages, so the above limitation or exclusion may not apply to you.

▶ A statement regarding the consumer's legal rights as follows:

This warranty gives you specific legal rights, and you may also have other rights which vary from state to state.

▶ Any limitations on the duration of *implied warranties*, together with this statement:

Some states do not allow limitations on how long an implied warranty lasts, so the above limitation may not apply to you.

Your Hidden Warranties and Strict Liabilities

Express warranties arise from statements you make about a product or service, from a picture, sample, or brochure, while *implied warranties* arise by automatic operation of law. Although the Magnuson–Moss Consumer Warranty Act supersedes state laws regarding *express warranties* in the sale of products (see above), it does not supersede the Uniform Commercial Code (UCC) provisions on *implied warranties* or state laws applicable to *express warranties* in the sale of services. Be aware of the following with regard to UCC provisions on *implied warranties:*

1. Two primary warranties are implied by the UCC, the *implied warranty of merchantability* and the *implied warranty of fitness for particular purpose.*

2. The *implied warranty of merchantability* is an unstated assurance that a particular product will be fit for the ordinary purposes for which it is used—for example, an automobile should run. Any *disclaimer* of this assurance must be prominently set forth in clear language that includes the word "merchantability."

3. The *implied warranty of fitness for particular purpose* is an unstated assurance that a product will be suitable for a purpose to which it will be put, based on available information. For example, if you know that a customer needs shoes for mountain climbing, your sale of a certain pair for that purpose creates a warranty of fitness. Any *disclaimer* of this assurance must be prominently set forth in clear language.

4. In the absence of a *disclaimer,* there are also *implied warranties* that a product does not infringe a patent and that you are transferring good title to it.

A *disclaimer* may wholly deny that you are making one or more express or implied warranties, or it may limit warranty coverages. In the absence of a *disclaimer,* a breach of warranty will usually give a purchaser of the item the right to recover the cost of the item together with any additional damages caused by that breach. For example, if there had been no disclaimer when you purchased a defective videocassette for your video-recording trip to Hawaii, the producer of the cassette could be required not only to give you a good cassette but also to give you another trip to Hawaii. But, if there had been a valid *disclaimer,* the producer could only be required to replace the cassette.

Many jurisdictions apply *strict liability* in holding sellers and manufacturers legally responsible for injuries resulting from design or manufacturing defects where neither negligence nor breach of warranty can be found. Such *strict liability* cases run into the millions each year. But the worst news is that sound marketing practices and disclaimers of warranty can do little to avoid *strict liability*—your only protection is the purchase of product liability insurance. What's more, the law labels the contractual limitation of damages for personal injuries from consumer goods as "unconscionable" and generally unenforceable.

Subject to the exceptions in connection with your *strict liability*, your responsibility for a product's repair or replacement and for damages of a commercial nature may be limited by a conspicuous and timely *disclaimer*, as previously discussed. Because the obligations imposed by law in the areas of warranty are so extensive, be sure to consult your attorney to develop the most fully effective *disclaimer* that is possible in your business. Exhibit 5-1 is an example of a limited warranty and disclaimer used in the sale of one line of goods.

A Few FTC Specifics

As we have seen, the philosophy of the FTC is to protect the consumer. The theory deserves some practical amplification. Note and avoid these specific practices, which the FTC has criticized:

1. *Implying that your product is manufactured by a "big corporation" unless it is.*
2. *Confusing your audience with misleading endorsements.* Claiming that "doctors recommend Vitamin–Tab" can only get you in trouble if the "doctor" you are quoting happens to be your brother-in-law.
3. *Fostering misunderstandings about your association with another concern.* Pretending that your repair shop is an official "major company" outlet is wishful thinking that can backfire.
4. *Exaggerating your product's benefits.* You will probably be able to sell your mouthwash just as well, even if it cannot cure the common cold.

Exhibit 5-1. Thirty-day limited warranty—price refund.

WARRANTY COVERAGE: All widgets from Widget Manufacturing Co., Inc., are warranted to be free from defects in material and workmanship. A refund of the price paid for widgets (excluding sales and use taxes) is available on certain conditions described below if the warranty is not met. THIS WARRANTY IS VOID IF THE WIDGET HAS BEEN DAMAGED BY ACCIDENT, UNREASONABLE USE, NEGLECT, IMPROPER SERVICE, OR OTHER CAUSES NOT ARISING OUT OF DEFECTS IN MATERIAL OR WORKMANSHIP.

THIS WARRANTY EXTENDS TO THE ORIGINAL CONSUMER PURCHASER OF A WIDGET AT PARTICIPATING DEALERS ONLY.

WARRANTY DURATION: Each widget is warranted to the original consumer purchaser for a period of thirty (30) days from the original purchase date.

WARRANTY DISCLAIMERS: ANY IMPLIED WARRANTIES ARISING OUT OF SALE OF A WIDGET, INCLUDING BUT NOT LIMITED TO THE IMPLIED WARRANTIES OF MERCHANTABILITY AND FITNESS FOR A PARTICULAR PURPOSE, ARE LIMITED IN DURATION TO THE ABOVE THIRTY-DAY PERIOD. WIDGET MANUFACTURING CO., INC., SHALL NOT BE LIABLE FOR LOSS OF USE OF THE PRODUCT OR OTHER INCIDENTAL OR CONSEQUENTIAL COSTS, EXPENSES, OR DAMAGES INCURRED BY THE CONSUMER OR ANY OTHER USER.
  Some states do not allow the exclusion or limitation of implied warranties or consequential damages, so the above limitations or exclusions may not apply to you.

LEGAL REMEDIES: This warranty gives you specific legal rights, and you may also have other rights that vary from state to state.

WARRANTY PERFORMANCE: During the above thirty-day warranty period, your refund (which will not exceed manufacturer's suggested retail price) will be remitted when your widget is sent postage or freight prepaid to the address listed below, together with the following:
  1. Proof-of-purchase, including the sales slip.
  2. Your signed statement describing the respects in which the warranty was not met.
The other conditions for such refund are that the widget be sent to the address below in its original packaging, including the packing materials, and that the shipment or mailing be insured for not less than the amount of refund being requested. Other than the postage requirement and nonrefund of sales and use taxes, no charge will be made for such refund.

Exhibit 5-1. *Continued*

WIDGET MANUFACTURING CO., INC., will confirm by telephone whether or not a particular vendor is a Participating Dealer if you call (000) 555-5555 during weekday business hours.

WIDGET MANUFACTURING CO., INC.
1 YOU-NAME-IT STREET
ANYCITY, ANYSTATE 00000

5. *Misrepresenting your product's origin.* Your "imports" had better be genuine.
6. *Labeling goods as "new" when they aren't.* A product is generally new for only six months.
7. *Contending that your product meets a standard unless you can prove it.* Avoid unequivocal words like "best," "colorfast," and "aged"; the consumer may have a right to take you literally.
8. *Misstating the quantity of goods available.* Your "limited supply" must be just that; otherwise, you are exercising undue pressure on the consumer.
9. *Disparaging a competitor.* "Commercial freedom of speech" encourages comparative advertising, but it demands a complete and accurate presentation.
10. *Advertising a loss leader without intending to meet a reasonable public demand unless you also communicate the fact that quantities are limited.*
11. *Advertising a "going-out-of-business sale" unless you are closing your doors.* And don't hold a "fire sale" unless you have suffered a fire.

5.03   Where Credit Is Due

Chapter 6 reviews the extensive federal requirements in the credit area, including some that are difficult to understand and implement correctly. Although an independent credit program may be essential or at least important for many small businesses, for others it may make a lot of sense to limit credit activities to accepting one or more of the nationally known credit cards. The commissions that the providers of these cards charge for their own administrative costs and profits may be less than the out-of-pocket costs you might incur in handling a credit program of your own; just preparing and mailing statements can be a major cost item. Also, the competition among the providers of the nationally known cards sometimes can lead to reductions in their commissions, a result that may depend in part on your negotiating leverage and abilities.

5.04 Product Safety and Other Regulations Galore

A business that makes or sells a *consumer product* should give high priority to complying 100 percent with the *Consumer Product Safety Act*. A *consumer product* covers both a finished article and its separate components if intended for use or usable in and around a permanent or temporary household or residence, a school, in recreation, or otherwise. The main requirements of this Act are to comply with consumer product safety rules promulgated by the Consumer Product Safety Commission and to notify the Commission in two situations, as follows:

1. You have reason to think a consumer product made or sold by you may cause a serious risk of injury. Such a product is, by definition, considered to have a "substantial product hazard."
2. You receive information indicating that a product made or sold by you fails to comply with an applicable consumer product safety rule.

This Act has both civil and criminal penalties for noncompliance; so if you make or sell consumer products, review the Commission's regulations with your attorney in an especially careful way.

Closely related to product safety are the developments in the product liability and product liability insurance areas. These developments dramatically underscore the need to make safe products and prominently display warnings of any hazards. As everyone knows, juries have been awarding increasingly enormous recoveries of damages for defective products or display of warnings, leading to:

- ▶ Reductions in the amount of coverage available under product liability insurance and, in many cases, to cancellations of such insurance and withdrawals of insurance companies from the underwriting of risks in this area.
- ▶ Establishment of subsidiary insurance companies by large manufacturers so that they can self-insure product liability risks economically.
- ▶ Legislative proposals to limit liability awards so that insurance companies and small manufacturers can compete in the product marketing field. Such proposals have largely been defeated even though the United Kingdom has had statutes in this area for over fifty years. Even the model product liability law developed by the U.S. Department of Commerce has been rejected by the state legislatures. The proponents of these proposals claim that both the victims recovering damage awards, and their contingent fee lawyers, have been overcompensated at the expense of both the public and the shareholders or other owners of manufacturing concerns. The other view is that it is not traditional in our legal system to limit arbitrarily the amount a jury can decide to award, a view supported vigorously by associations of trial/plaintiff attorneys.

In view of these developments, it is an essential first step for anyone considering the marketing of virtually any products, whether as a manufacturer, distributor, or retailer, to engage counsel experienced in the product liability field. No product categories are immune—clothing may be too flammable, for example, or the ink used in books or periodicals may contain excessively toxic chemicals.

The FTC has issued many regulations applicable to businesses generally that are both complex and voluminous. They are all available from the Bureau of Information, Federal Trade Commission,

Washington, D.C. 20580. Be sure to stay on the safe side by becoming aware of the following:

▶ Many state laws—notably the *Uniform Deceptive Trade Practice and Consumer Protection Act*—pick up where FTC guidelines leave off. False and misleading advertising thus becomes the rightful prey of two levels of government.

▶ The states also regulate the advertisement of securities, banks, professions, insurance—you name it. One of the areas most extensively regulated by the states is the sale of new automobiles. So-called lemon laws give consumer purchasers of defective cars a number of repair and refund rights that override the terms of any warranty *disclaimer* (see section 5.02).

▶ Federal postal laws prohibit using the mails to perpetuate a fraud, transmit alcoholic beverages or obscene or lascivious matter, incite certain crimes, or promote lotteries. Remember that almost all newspapers and magazines are distributed through the mail, thus subjecting their contents to postal inquiry.

▶ The federal government has all kinds of special powers to regulate particular industries, and that power is broadly exercised. The IRS, for instance, regulates the advertising of alcoholic beverages; the Federal Communications Commission regulates radio and TV broadcasts; the Securities and Exchange Commission regulates the advertising of stocks and bonds.

▶ Ads are subject to slander and libel laws. Be sure of your facts and your legal authority to use them.

▶ The *Robinson–Patman Act* prohibits a seller from paying a buyer for a service the buyer furnishes unless that payment is also made available to the buyer's competitors. A seller may not discriminate in favor of one buyer over another. So cooperative advertising programs ought to be made known equally to all competing customers.

▶ Lotteries, which involve prizes, consideration, and chance, may constitute unfair competition under both federal and state laws

and be subject to state regulations on gambling. That is why advertisers using such promotional devices seek to avoid either consideration ("no purchase need be made") or chance ("duplicate prizes
will be awarded in the event of a tie").

Handling the Free-Lancer

Once you decide what your ad may say and what it may not, the
remaining legal objective is your protection in disseminating that
information. First, you should clarify your relationship with any
artist, copywriter, or photographer you hire. Before ink is put to
paper, have your lawyer draft a simple letter agreement covering
these points:

► A warranty by your contractor that everything he submits to
   you is his own work.
► Your legal rights over any material your contractor develops
   on your time. Have him specifically assign his rights in any
   creative work he speculatively developed for you before you
   hired him.
► An acknowledgment of your exclusive right to copyright your
   contractor's work (see section 4.04).
► That you are the sole arbiter of what is acceptable work and
   what is not.
► A requirement that releases be obtained before pictures or
   testimonials are used. Invasion of privacy can give rise to a
   lawsuit.

Your Contract With the Media

After an ad is developed, the publishing or broadcasting of it
creates additional rights and obligations. As an advertiser, you will
be called upon to present your title to all material you submit. You
will agree to submit copy and artwork and to pay for your ad on
time. Finally, you will be expected to avoid statements that violate
FTC and similar standards.

Here is what the media is obligated to do for you:

- ▶ Provide time and space in a fair and impartial manner.
- ▶ Charge equal and fair rates to all advertisers. A couple of exceptions: Frequency discounts and long-run discounts are permitted: so are surcharges for short-term runs.
- ▶ Perform accurately. The media can be held liable for your out-of-pocket loss and any loss in goodwill that results from their errors. However, liability is uniformly limited by contract to a small dollar amount, and you are obligated to mitigate whatever damage you suffer.

Hiring an Agency

Many companies assume still another contractual relationship in advertising their products—retaining an advertising agency. Unfortunately, the creative professionalism you can buy in an agency accomplishes little in the way of exculpation for the advertising sins this chapter has explored. As the principal, your company retains ultimate control over your agent and, with it, ultimate liability for whatever your agent does and says on your behalf. Most agencies are painstaking in preserving their good names by ensuring fairness and honesty in all they present to the public, but you will remain responsible for your ad's contents. That being the case, what legal protections of competency are you actually guaranteed?

- ▶ *Expertise.* You have a legal right to your agency's best efforts and greatest skill.
- ▶ *Loyalty.* Your interests come first. That means that your trade secrets (section 4.03) are not to be divulged and that any useful information your agency learns is to be brought to your attention. It makes sense, then, that your agency may not represent the competition unless both you and your competitor agree.
- ▶ *Obedience.* You have a right to your agent's full cooperation. All your instructions should be carried out unless they are illegal or clearly unreasonable.
- ▶ *Fiduciary responsibility.* Your agent may not "self-deal," nor may it unilaterally contract out your work to another of its

clients. What is more, any expense money you deposit with your agent must be segregated and used to pay only the bills you authorize, not the agent's general debts.

▶ *Fiscal honesty.* Your agent is obliged to render frequent and strict accountings to you.

The Agency Contract

These principles take on practical significance in the formal contract between agent and client. The agency contract's major provisions should include the following:

▶ *A description of the services the agency is to perform and its fee for those services.* Note the way fees are computed: Are they straight commissions, media cost plus an incremental percentage of media costs for profit, or media cost plus an hourly rate? Or what?

▶ *Disbursement guidelines.* What authority is required prior to an expense payout? To whom should disbursements be made?

▶ *Status reports and approval.* Do you retain the right to approve each component within a campaign?

▶ *Deadlines.* Are they realistic and do they conform to the seasonal nature of your business?

▶ *Billing procedures.* Do payment dates reasonably correspond to completion dates? What credit terms, if any, are you given?

▶ *Discounts.* Does the agency agree to take advantage of all discounts and pass the savings on to the advertiser?

▶ *The ownership of ideas.* Is the advertiser acknowledged as the sole owner of all material developed, even of that which isn't used?

▶ *Fiduciary duties.* Are they all spelled out?

▶ *Indemnification.* Where the advertiser and agency may be jointly liable, would you be compelled to hold the agency harmless?

▶ *Term.* What is the duration of the contract? How much notice must be given to terminate it?

5.05   A Personal Code

Only the most naïve will assert that the statutory law of the marketplace and its morality are one. Yet, to grow successfully, you will not need legal clearance for every advertising and marketing idea that comes your way. Simply apply your own standards of fairness and honesty, and, except for the most technical points, your legal judgment will match your lawyer's.

6 Giving Them Credit

Ready money is Aladdin's Lamp.

—Lord Byron

6.01 Expanding Your Profit Base

The extension of retail credit is frequently an indispensable adjunct to the sales effort. If your goods and services could be bought only by cash or on a nationally known credit card, you could stand to lose customers. Rather than turn that business away, you might prefer to establish your own credit and collection program, retaining the charge customers that you might otherwise lose and gaining additional profit from permissible finance charges on your receivables.

The principles of full disclosure and other fair treatment apply extensively in the area of credit, where five federal statutes lay down a large number of specific requirements.

The *Truth-in-Lending Act* (TIL), originally adopted in 1968 and since amended more than five times, demands standardized formats and language in the advertisement of all consumer credit (except in connection with student loans, where similar but different rules apply). Advertisements of credit terms are regulated in part by the Federal Trade Commission (FTC), but more substantially by the Federal Reserve Board under its Regulation Z, which imposes these restrictions:

▶ To protect the consumer from "bait" advertising, an advertiser is prohibited from offering to extend credit to buyers unless he customarily arranges such terms.

▶ An advertiser may not offer "no down payment" or any specific down payment unless he will accept those terms.

▶ Any advertisement that seeks to promote credit, but where the seller is not imposing a specific finance charge, must clearly state that "the cost of credit is included in the price quoted for the goods and services." Any ad that does refer to a finance charge or any other credit term (such as a down-payment or repayment period) must provide a specific annual percentage rate (APR), using those precise words and figures calculated in accordance with a mandatory computation system that takes up many pages of the *Code of Federal Regulations*—and is still difficult to understand.

▶ Any ad offering open-end credit (including revolving charge accounts and credit cards) must comply with your state's usury law and "clearly and conspicuously" disclose:
1. The finance charge APRs and the range of unpaid balances to which these rates will be applied
2. The time period, if any, within which the balance may be paid off without a finance charge
3. The method used to compute finance charges and the range of balances to which they are applied

▶ Any ad offering loans or installment sales must comply with your state's usury law and must "clearly and conspicuously" disclose:
1. The cash price or the amount of the loan
2. The amount of the finance charge, given as an APR
3. The amount of the down payment, or that no down payment is required
4. The number, amount, and date of repayments
5. The deferred payment price or the sum of the payments, whichever applies

In addition to the TIL, you still need to consider four other federal credit laws, which are enforced by the FTC:

1. *The Fair Debt Collection Practices Act.* This Act provides that if you go beyond any one of a number of limitations in your efforts to collect payment from customers, the customers

can acquire rights to monetary damages from you over and above what they owe. Be sure to use an experienced attorney or collection agency to enforce your rights.

2. *The Fair Credit Billing Act.* The ways in which you bill customers, and handle their questions about and objections to your statements, are subject to detailed regulations by the FTC.

3. *The Fair Credit Reporting Act.* Under this statute, each of your credit customers has the right to examine his credit file and to have changes, additions, and deletions made if the file might unfairly affect any future extension of credit.

4. *The Equal Credit Opportunity Act.* This law basically ensures women of treatment equivalent to that given men when applying for credit, with legal rights to recover against a business that does not comply with the requirements.

6.02   Limiting Your Exposure

The first step in the consumer credit process is screening the credit applicant. Your selectivity in accepting credit risks is crucial to the eventual collection of monies owed you. The Equal Credit Opportunity Act sees to it that your selectivity is rational by setting these rules:

1. You may not discount the income your applicant draws from part-time employment.

2. You may not seek information about an applicant's spouse unless the spouse is to share the benefits and responsibilities of the account; now, you must maintain separate credit histories for both a husband and wife who share an account.

3. You may not deny credit on the basis of sex or marital status.

The mass preselection of credit risks has rightfully been replaced by individual investigations into the creditworthiness of applicants. The Fair Credit Reporting Act, designed principally to regulate consumer reporting agencies, applies equally to those who request the investigative reports. Before using an investigative report, you are obliged to let your applicant know:

1. That an investigative report may be used.
2. Just what an investigative report is.
3. That he has a right to request a "complete and accurate" statement describing the type and scope of the investigation conducted. (If he exercises this right, you have five days to comply with his request.)

Exhibit 6-1 is an example of an FTC form designed for making those disclosures.

If a credit report discloses information that causes you to deny a credit request or to increase the charge for credit, you must so advise your customer and supply him with the name and address of the agency responsible for the project. He can then challenge the completeness or accuracy of the information you have received. If a source other than a credit bureau has forwarded information that influences you to decide against the applicant, again he can challenge the information. Let the applicant know that credit is denied and that he may request in writing the nature of the information that led to your decision. The FTC suggests the format shown in Exhibit 6-2.

Exhibit 6-1. Disclosure of investigative consumer report.

[When a separate notice is used]
[This is to inform you that as part of our procedure for processing your credit application]

[or]

[When disclosed in the application]
[In making this application for credit it is understood that]
an investigation may be made whereby information is obtained through personal interviews with your neighbors, friends, or others with whom you are acquainted. This inquiry includes information as to your character, general reputation, personal characteristics, and mode of living. You have the right to make a written request within a reasonable period of time to receive additional, detailed information about the nature and scope of this investigation.

Exhibit 6-2. Nature of information disclosure.

[*date*]

Mr. Harry Doe
615 Avenue "B"
Anytown, USA 00000

Dear Mr. Doe:

In response to your request for a statement of our reasons for turning down your recent application for credit, our records reveal that your application was not approved because:

[Your employer informed us that you were a part-time rather than full-time employee.]

[*or*]

[A department store in this city told us that you were several months behind on your payments.]

[*or*]

[The local branch office of a finance company informed us that it had turned your account with them over to a collection agency.]

[*or*]

[A bank in this city told us that your checking account was consistently overdrawn.]

We appreciate your patronage, and invite you to shop with us on a cash basis.

Very truly yours,

Richard Roe,
Credit Manager

6.03   The Pervasive Regulation Z

Your credit customers may be protected by your state's Uniform Consumer Credit Code (UCCC) on an even broader basis than that provided under Regulation Z. Where enacted, the UCCC takes the place of federal law; it deserves special study, along with all the other state legislation that will control your credit program.

In most states, however, Regulation Z is the major source of requirements applicable to the operation of consumer credit programs. It applies to any individual or organization that "extends or arranges credit for which a finance charge is or may be payable or which is repayable by agreement in more than four installments," but not to you if your customers unilaterally decide to pay your bills piecemeal. Nearly all kinds of credit are subject to the Regulation except these:

▶ Commercial and business credit
▶ Credit to (but not from) federal, state, and local governments
▶ Transactions in securities and commodities with broker-dealers who are registered with the SEC
▶ Non–real estate credit over $25,000
▶ Student loans and agricultural credit transactions

Apart from these exceptions, virtually all credit transactions require full disclosure of the true costs of credit. Following are your obligations as a creditor complying with Regulation Z:

1. You must adopt the specific language and disclosure forms the Regulation prescribes, making a number of disclosures before the credit transaction is consummated.

2. You must maintain your credit records for at least two years.

3. You must state the annual percentage rate of finance charge to the nearest ⅛ of one percent, using the words "annual percentage rate." If periodic or variable rates are used, additional requirements apply to the manner of disclosure.

4. You must disclose the full finance charge your customer pays for credit, including these (see section 6.05):

- ▶ Interest
- ▶ Any loan fee
- ▶ Any finder's fee
- ▶ Any time-price differential
- ▶ Any amount paid as a discount
- ▶ Any service, transaction, or carrying charge
- ▶ Any "points," or prepaid interest
- ▶ Any investigation, credit report, or appraisal fee in a non–real estate transaction
- ▶ The premium for credit-life, health, and accident insurance if it is a condition for giving credit

5. Residential mortgage transactions require granting a right of rescission within three days.

6. Credit balances for both open-end and closed-end credit must be properly treated.

7. For open-end credit, payments must be credited promptly, periodic statements must be sent regularly, and proper disclosures must be made as to credit card provisions and billing error rights.

Section 105(b) of the revised TIL requires the Federal Reserve Board to publish model forms and clauses, which the Fed has made available together with certain other appendices as follows:

[*Most model forms and clauses appear in the appendices indicated by asterisks below.*]

Appendix A: Effect on state laws
Appendix B: State exemptions
Appendix C: Issuance of staff interpretations
Appendix D: Multiple-advance construction loans
Appendix E: Rules for card issuers that bill on a transaction-by transaction basis
*Appendix F: Annual percentage rate computations for certain open-end credit plans
*Appendix G: Open-end model forms and clauses
*Appendix H: Closed-end model forms and clauses
Appendix I: Federal enforcement agencies

*Appendix J: Annual percentage rate computations for closed-end credit transactions

All of these appendices are available from the U.S. Government Printing Office, Washington, D.C. 20402.

"Open-End" Disclosures

Regulation Z divides credit into two categories and deals with each separately. The first is *open-end credit*, defined as a credit transaction in which a finance charge is added to the customer's unpaid balance each month. You are obliged to provide all the following information before your customer's first open-end charge transaction takes place:

▶ *The conditions for imposing a finance charge and the period during which payment can be made without incurring a finance charge.* Of course, you are always free to extend any grace period without notice.

▶ *The method used to determine the balance against which a finance charge will be imposed each month.* You have various choices, such as (1) considering the previous balance (outstanding for half the billing cycle), (2) using the adjusted previous balance (subtracting the payments made this month from the amount owed last month), or (3) looking at the average daily balance (adding each day's balance and dividing the total by the number of days in the cycle). Even periodic or variable rates may be used, provided proper disclosures and calculation methods for finance charge are used.

▶ *The way the actual finance charge is calculated.*

▶ *The periodic rates used and the range of balance to which each applies.*

▶ *The conditions under which any additional charges may be made and the way such charges would be calculated.* If charges are made based on specific transactions, then the APR tables set forth in the Fed's Appendix F (see p. 104) should be used—but most open-end credit plans do not involve such charges.

- ▸ A description of any lien that may be acquired on a customer's property.
- ▸ The minimum payment due each month.
- ▸ A statement of the customer's rights to dispute billing errors under the Fair Credit Billing Act, substantially similar to the model notice in the Fed's Appendix G (see p. 104). Your adapted statement might resemble the one in Exhibit 6-3.

After an account is opened, you must issue periodic statements if there is any finance charge imposed or if there is a debit or credit balance exceeding one dollar. Those statements should be patterned after the Fed's Appendix G (see p. 104), and might be similar to Exhibit 6-4. Exhibit 6-4 is an example of a retailer's statement, prepared by a manual billing operation, for an account on which the finance charge is determined by a single periodic rate or a minimum charge of 50 cents applicable to balances under a specific amount. It also assumes that the finance charge is computed on the previous balance before deducting payments and/or credits. Separate slips must accompany each statement, identifying all charges and credits and showing the dates and amounts thereof.

In your statements to credit customers, be sure to provide all the following information, to the extent applicable:

- ▸ The debit or credit balance at the start of the billing period.
- ▸ Identification of each purchase transaction by date, name and address of vendor, and transaction number; alternatively, copies of all sales vouchers.
- ▸ Dates and amounts of customer payments, and of any returns, credits, or adjustments.
- ▸ The "annual percentage rate" (using that term), which can be variable and is referred to as the periodic rate in the required disclosure of the *balance computation method*.
- ▸ The *balance computation method*, which can be disclosed in accordance with any one of four model clauses as follows:

    Adjusted Balance Method
    We figure [a portion of] the finance charge on your account by applying the periodic rate to the "adjusted balance" of your account. We get the "adjusted balance" by taking the balance you owed at the end of the previous billing cycle and subtracting [any

Exhibit 6-3. Notice of billing error rights.

This notice contains important information about your rights and our responsibilities under the Fair Credit Billing Act.

YOUR BILLING RIGHTS: KEEP THIS NOTICE FOR FUTURE USE

If you think your bill is wrong, or if you need more information about a transaction on your bill, write us separately at the address listed on your bill. Write to us as soon as possible. We must hear from you no later than 60 days after we send you the first bill on which the error or problem appears. You can telephone us, but doing so will not preserve your rights. In your letter, give us the following information:

- ▶ Your name and account number (if any).
- ▶ The dollar amount of the suspected error.
- ▶ A description of the error. Explain, if you can, why you believe there is an error. If you need more information, describe the item you are not sure about.

If you have authorized us to pay your credit card bill automatically from your savings or checking account, you can stop the payment of any amount you think is wrong. To stop the payment, your letter must reach us three business days before the automatic payment is scheduled to occur.

YOUR RIGHTS AND OUR RESPONSIBILITIES
AFTER WE RECEIVE YOUR WRITTEN NOTICE

We must acknowledge your letter within 30 days, unless we have corrected the error by then. Within 90 days, we must either correct the error or explain why we believe the bill was correct.

After we receive your letter, we cannot try to collect any amount you question or report you as delinquent. We can continue to bill you for the amount you question, including finance charges, and we can apply any unpaid amount against your credit limit. You do not have to pay any questioned amount while we are investigating, but you are still obligated to pay the parts of the your bill that are not in question.

If we find that we made a mistake on your bill, you will not have to pay any finance charges related to any questioned amount. If we didn't make a mistake, you may have to pay finance charges, and you will have to make up any missed payments on the questioned amount. In either case, we will send you a statement of the amount you owe and the date that it is due.

If you fail to pay the amount that we think you owe, we may report you as delinquent. However, if our explanation does not satisfy you and you write to us within ten days telling us that you still refuse to pay, we must tell anyone we report you to that you have a question about your bill. And, we must tell you the name of anyone we reported you to. We must tell anyone we report you to that the matter has been settled between us when it finally is.

(continued)

Exhibit 6-3. *Continued*

If we don't follow these rules, we can't collect the first $50 of the questioned amount, even if your bill was correct.

SPECIAL RULE FOR CREDIT CARD PURCHASES

If you have a problem with the quality of goods or services that you purchased from us with a credit card, and you have tried in good faith to correct the problem with the merchant, you may not have to pay the remaining amount due on the goods or services. There are two limitations on this right:

    (1) You must have made the purchase in your home state or, if not within your home state, within 100 miles of your current mailing address; and

    (2) The purchase price must have been more than $50.

These limitations do not apply if we own or operate the merchant or if we mailed you the advertisement for the property or services.

---

unpaid finance charges and] any payments and credits received during the present billing cycle.

Previous Balance Method

We figure [a portion of] the finance charge on your account by applying the periodic rate to the amount you owe at the beginning of each billing cycle [minus any unpaid finance charges]. We do not subtract any payments or credits received during the billing cycle. [The amount of payments and credits to your account this billing cycle was $_____.]

Average Daily Balance Method [excluding current transactions]

We figure [a portion of] the finance charge on your account by applying the periodic rate to the "average daily balance" of your account [excluding current transactions]. To get the "average daily balance," we take the beginning balance of your account each day and subtract any payments or credits [and any unpaid finance charges]. We do not add in any new [purchases/advances/ loans]. This gives us the daily balance. Then, we add all the daily balances for the billing cycle together and divide the total by the number of days in the billing cycle. This gives us the "average daily balance."

Average Daily Balance Method [including current transactions]

We figure [a portion of] the finance charge on your account by applying the periodic rate to the "average daily balance" of your

Exhibit 6-4. Example retailer's statement.

ANYSTORE U.S.A.
Main Street, Anycity, U.S.A.
Direct customer inquiries to the attention of Mr. John Smith.

[Customer's name here]

AMT. PAID $_____

TO ENSURE PROPER CREDIT, RETURN THIS PORTION WITH YOUR PAYMENT.

PREVIOUS BALANCE	*FINANCE CHARGE 50 CENTS MINIMUM*	*PAYMENTS*	*CREDITS*	*PURCHASES*	*NEW BALANCE*	*MINIMUM PAYMENT*

Finance Charge is Computed by a "Periodic Rate" of _____% per month (or a minimum charge of 50 cents for balances under $_____), which is annual percentage rate of _____% applied to the previous balance without deducting current payments and/or credits appearing on this statement.

Notice
Please see accompanying statement(s) for important information.

Payments, credits, or charges, received after the date shown above the arrow, which is the closing date of this billing cycle, will appear on your next statement. To avoid additional finance charges, pay the "new balance" before this date next month.

Anystore, USA, Main Street, Anycity, USA

account [including current transactions]. To get the "average daily balance," we take the beginning balance of your account each day, add any new [purchases/advances/loans], and subtract any payments or credits [and unpaid finance charges]. This gives us the daily balance. Then, we add up all the daily balances for the billing cycle and divide the total by the number of days in the billing cycle. This gives us the "average daily balance."

► The finance charge in dollars and cents.
► The billing cycle's closing date and the balance at that time.
► An address for customer inquiries.
► A statement of the customer's rights under the Fair Credit Billing Act, unless you semiannually send the more comprehensive statement of rights in the event of a billing dispute. Your statement of billing rights might resemble Exhibit 6-3, but most credit operators print an abbreviated version of Exhibit 6-3 on the reverse side of their billing statements.

Telling All—About Loans and Installment Sales

The second category of credit as provided by Regulation Z includes all other credit transactions—loans, installment sales, and any excursion of credit for a specified period, where the total amount and due dates are understood on day one. Those transactions do not fall under the open-end rules, and they require the following disclosures in writing before they can be consummated:

► *The "amount financed," using that term, and a brief description such as "the amount of credit provided to you or on your behalf."* Although any down payment and prepaid finance charge must be subtracted from the amount financed, other amounts that are financed must be included.

► *The total "finance charge," using that term, in dollars and cents.*

► *The "annual percentage rate," using that term.* However, if the finance charge is less than $5 on credit under $75 or less than $7.50 on credit over $75, the APR need not be disclosed. In calculating the APR, payments must first be applied to interest and then to principal. APR tables are set forth in the Fed's Appendix J (see p. 104). If the rate is variable and may increase, disclosure must be made of the circumstances under which the rate may increase, any limitations on the increase, and the effect of the increase, and an example must be given regarding the payment terms that would result from an increase.

▶ *The payment schedule, or the number, amounts, and timing of payments scheduled to repay the obligation.* If the payments amounts vary, the schedule must show the dollar amounts of the largest and smallest payments in the series and refer to the variations in the other payments in the series.

▶ *The "total of payments," using that term, and a descriptive explanation such as "the amount you will have paid when you have made all scheduled payments."*

▶ *Other disclosures, depending on the type of transaction.* These include any demand feature, the "total sale price" (for sale/credit transactions), prepayment right and any applicable penalty, late payment charges, any security interest taken, insurance provisions, and a statement that the consumer should refer to the appropriate contract document for information about nonpayment, default, the right to accelerate the maturity of the obligation, and prepayment rebates and penalties. If it is a residential mortgage transaction, there must be a statement about whether a subsequent purchaser can assume the remaining obligations. If a deposit is required, there must be a statement that the APR does not reflect the effect of the required deposit.

The model closed-end disclosure form included in the Fed's Appendix H (see p. 104) should be your guide in developing these disclosures.

6.04 Supplemental Disclosures

A *refinancing* or *assumption* subsequent to the initial closed-end refinancing triggers new TIL disclosure requirements.

A *refinancing* occurs when an existing closed-end obligation is satisfied and is replaced by a new obligation of the same consumer. Although a deferral of individual installments isn't a refinancing, any other rescheduling of payments is, and so are debt consolidations and disbursements of new money. A refinancing is treated as a new transaction requiring disclosures based on the facts at that time, not the facts prevailing at the time of the initial transaction. Unless a simple interest method has been used to compute the finance charges in the initial transaction, a refinancing will result in a requirement of a rebate of unearned charges under most state laws, since the transaction is considered to be a type of prepayment. If the unearned charges are not credited against the outstanding obligations, TIL requires that they be ,added to and disclosed as finance charges in the new transaction.

Assumptions relate only to existing residential mortgage transactions, but contract purchases and even mobile home purchase loans are covered if residential abodes are involved. There is an assumption if there is a written agreement and an express acceptance of a successor obligor by the creditor. If you do not expressly accept the new obligor, but state in writing that the initial obligor remains the primary obligor, the required disclosures for assumptions do not apply—even though you may mail the new party a coupon book or notice to pay.

6.05   What's In, and Not In, the Finance Charge

Properly computing the *finance charge* is the key to complying with the most difficult part of TIL and Regulation Z, and just determining the charges that are included and excluded can be the hardest part of all. To determine whether an item is part of the finance charge, compare your charges in a credit transaction with those payable in a similar cash transaction; those charges imposed uniformly in both types of transactions are not part of the finance charge. However, if the amount is greater in the credit transaction, then the difference is part of the finance charge.

For example, the following are part of the finance charge:

- ▶ Inspection and handling fees for disbursement of construction loan proceeds at various stages
- ▶ Fee for preparing a TIL disclosure statement
- ▶ Charges for a required maintenance or service contract if applicable only in a credit transaction
- ▶ Points, loan fees, assumption fees, finder's fees, and similar charges
- ▶ Appraisal, investigation, and credit report fees, unless the transaction is a residential mortgage transaction and the fees are bona fide and reasonable in amount
- ▶ Charges for any guaranty or insurance covering default or credit losses
- ▶ Charges for credit life, accident, health, or loss-of-income insurance, or casualty or liability insurance

On the other hand, the following are not part of the finance charge:

- ▶ Application fees charged to all applicants for credit, whether or not credit is actually extended
- ▶ Late payment and similar charges
- ▶ Fees charged for participation in a credit plan, whether assessed on an annual or other periodic basis
- ▶ Seller's points
- ▶ Bona fide and reasonable fees in transactions secured by real property for:
  —Title examination, abstract of title, title insurance, settlement, and similar documents
  —Preparing deeds and mortgages and reconveyance settlement, and similar documents
  —Notary, appraisal, and credit reports

6.06 How Real Estate Credit Is Different

Real estate transactions follow the general rules for credit sales, but are subject to special legislation. Note these provisions in particular:

▶ You need not show the total dollar amount of the finance charge on a credit sale or first mortgage when the purchase is the customer's dwelling.

▶ When the customer's residence is used as collateral for credit (except for a first mortgage), he has the right to cancel the transaction by letter or telegram within three business days and get all his money back. This right may be waived only under extraordinary circumstances, and must be explained using the language shown in the Fed's model notice of right of rescission as set forth in its Appendix H (see section 6.03).

6.07 Playing Your Cards Right

There may be great appeal in sidestepping the problems of credit-risk evaluation and the billing and collecting process by using a nationally recognized credit card program (see section 5.04). The ease of prepackaged forms and the advertising advantage of the logo for Visa or MasterCard (or whatever) have forced many small-business owners to the same conclusion. The idea may well make sense for you. But before joining their ranks, consider the obligations you must undertake:

1. First you must pay a percentage of your monthly credit sales as the card company's fee, and pay it promptly. The issuer has the corresponding duty of billing and collecting for all valid card sales.

2. In addition, you may be asked to pay a nominal rental fee for use of the issuer's equipment. But expect all the proper forms to be free.

3. You are forced to honor any valid card, so anticipate a big drop in cash sales. The issuer cannot, however, prevent you from offering a discount for cash sales.

4. You are prohibited from honoring any suspicious cards, and are called upon to inform the issuer of your suspicions.

5. You are required to forward all sales slips and credit slips to the issuer within seven business days. After that, it's the issuer's responsibility.

6. Finally, you will be expected to indemnify the issuer from any claims resulting from defects in the goods you sell or in the services you render (see section 6.10).

6.08   The Forms Game

So the credit game is a forms game. The intelligent development and maintenance of your credit forms will ensure your legal compliance as you expand into new markets from your existing customer base. Legal ends and business ends should merge, so that with the analytical capacity that a forms system inevitably fosters, you should reach a new high in controlling the targets of your sales and, with that control, the collectibility of your profit.

Work with your lawyer to develop a systemized approach to consumer law compliance. Forms design and redesign will become a continuing, but worthwhile, demand as regulations—both federal and state—tighten and broaden. You should gain some additional knowledge of the way your business is affected right now by writing to the enforcement agency to which you are accountable. You will find the address in Exhibit 6-5, which lists the federal agency that covers your particular business. Any questions you have should be directed to that agency. These agencies are also responsible for enforcing Regulation Z. Your lawyer will keep you abreast of changes in the law that might force you to alter the way you conduct your company's credit policy.

6.09   A Collection Philosophy

However sophisticated your credit evaluation procedure may be, a fraction of your receivables will prove difficult to collect. Bad receivables are an unavoidable cost of doing credit business, a cost

Exhibit 6-5. Federal enforcement agencies.

NATIONAL BANKS

Office of Customer and Community Programs
Comptroller of the Currency
Washington, D.C. 20219

STATE MEMBER BANKS

Federal Reserve Bank serving the area in which the state member bank is located

NONMEMBER INSURED BANKS

Federal Deposit Insurance Corporation (FDIC) regional director for the region in which the nonmember insured bank is located

SAVINGS INSTITUTIONS INSURED BY THE FEDERAL·SAVINGS AND LOAN INSURANCE CORPORATION (FSLIC) AND MEMBER OF THE FEDERAL HOME LOAN BANK (FHLB) SYSTEM (EXCEPT FOR SAVINGS BANKS INSURED BY FDIC)

The FHLB Board's supervisory agent in the FHLB district in which the institution is located

FEDERAL CREDIT UNIONS

Regional office of the National Credit Union Administration serving the area in which the federal credit union is located

CREDITORS SUBJECT TO CIVIL AERONAUTICS BOARD

Director, Bureau of Consumer Protection
Civil Aeronautics Board
1825 Connecticut Avenue, N.W.
Washington, D.C. 20428

Exhibit 6-5. *Continued*

CREDITORS SUBJECT TO PACKERS AND STOCKYARDS ACT

Nearest Packers and Stockyards Administration Area supervisor

FEDERAL LOAN BANKS, FEDERAL LAND BANK ASSOCIATIONS, FEDERAL
INTERMEDIATE CREDIT BANKS, AND PRODUCTION CREDIT ASSOCIATIONS

Farm Credit Administration
490 L'Enfant Plaza, S.W.
Washington, D.C. 20578

RETAIL DEPARTMENT STORES, CONSUMER FINANCE COMPANIES, ALL
OTHER CREDITORS, AND ALL NONBANK CREDIT CARD ISSUERS

Division of Credit Practices
Bureau of Consumer Protection
Federal Trade Commission
Washington, D.C. 20580

---

well justified by the large majority of credit customers, who will
meet their obligations to you without so much as a reminder.

Efficient credit management dictates the creation of still another system of forms, the strong and straightforward series of collection notices that will help you turn receivables into cash. It is
the cumulative effect of the notices that will yield results. You
should review carefully the *Fair Debt Collection Practices Act*
(FDCPA), which prohibits many specific practices in collecting
debts, enables the FTC to seek penalties of up to $10,000 for each
violation, and gives consumers access to the federal courts for adjudication of their allegations of noncompliance. Within five days
after initial communication with a consumer, he must be given notice showing the amount owed and the name of the party to whom
it is owed. The FDCPA provides as follows:

1. You are prohibited from communicating with consumers at
unusual or inconvenient times or places, the presumption being
that any time before 8:00 A.M. or after 9:00 P.M. is inconvenient.
Communication may not be made to the consumer's place of em-

ployment if you know or have reason to know that his employer disapproves of such communication; and if you know the consumer is represented by counsel, then no communication to the consumer is allowed.

2. Once the consumer gives you written notice that he wants communications stopped, then only one more communication is permitted, to state what specific action will or may be taken.

3. Except for location information, communications with third parties (except, for example, family members and legal representatives) are prohibited.

4. You may not engage in any conduct, the natural consequence of which is to harass, oppress, or abuse any person. The FDCPA makes specific reference to repeated telephone calls with the intent to annoy, abuse, or harass the person called. If the tone of a letter is one of intimidation, lawsuits have held these prohibitions to have been violated.

5. Any contract placing debt-collection jurisdiction in courts distant from the debtor is prohibited.

6. Other prohibitions apply to false or misleading representations and to "any unfair or unconscionable means to collect a debt."

The obvious message of the FDCPA is that you can't be overzealous in your collection effort or you may unwittingly find yourself in violation of the law by overstating your collection message. Use restraint. Appeal to the debtor's sense of pride, fair play, and self-interest. Your integrity is far more valuable than any debt due you, so respect existing law on this matter.

Remember the following points:

1. *Avoid deceit.* You're not seeking information in connection with a survey, and you don't have a prepaid package for the debtor. Disguising your purpose of holding out an inducement to debtors to furnish information they would not voluntarily furnish can only backfire.

2. *Say who you are.* Creating the impression that you are a gov-

ernment agency, a credit bureau, or a collection agency is forbidden unless, of course, it's true.

3. *Above all, refrain from threats.* Deceptive debt collection practices might give rise to lawsuits on grounds including libel, extortion, mental anguish, and invasion of privacy, in addition to the sanctions already mentioned for violations of the FDCPA. Be straightforward but firm in your collection contracts. When all other attempts at collection fail, you may choose to exercise lawful "self-help" or refer the account to a reputable collection agency or, ultimately, to an attorney.

6.10 Where Due Process Stops You

Due process doctrines and consumer-oriented legislation place severe limitations on your recourses as a creditor. Be aware of developments involving credit collection practices, including the restrictions as follows:

▶ Your unauthorized entry onto a debtor's premises for purposes of repossession is generally prohibited by the Uniform Commercial Code (UCC or Code) as a "breach of the peace." Even though you may, for instance, repossess an automobile on a public road (if the debtor does not object), you may be held liable for any personal property within the car you repossess, and any protest by the debtor may preclude repossession altogether.

▶ Any goods you do repossess will almost certainly need to be resold after notice to the debtor, at a "commercially reasonable" sale. Otherwise, you are subject to both damages and penalties.

▶ You may not retain a "lay-away" deposit as liquidated damages after a customer's default; the practice has been labeled "unconscionable" by the courts.

▶ Both prior notice to the debtor and a hearing are required for wage garnishments and for the *replevin* (that is, the recovery of possession) of household goods.

▶ Another of the FTC's promulgations severely limits the use of negotiable instruments and so-called "waiver-of-defense" clauses in consumer contracts.

Today, all consumer credit contracts must clearly state in 10-point boldface type:

> ANY HOLDER OF THIS CONSUMER CREDIT CONTRACT IS SUBJECT TO ALL CLAIMS AND DEFENSES WHICH THE DEBTOR COULD AS-SERT AGAINST THE SELLER OF GOODS AND SERVICES OBTAINED PURSUANT HERETO OR WITH THE PROCEEDS HEREOF. RECOVERY HEREUNDER BY THE DEBTOR SHALL NOT EXCEED AMOUNTS PAID BY THE DEBTOR HEREUNDER.

A seller can no longer discount his customer's note to a finance company and be safe in the expectation that his customer will be forced to pay the finance company, even if the goods or services he sold prove defective. The finance company will be held responsible and will, in turn, hold the seller responsible. Although the rule excludes credit card transactions, the Fair Credit Billing Act invalidates "waivers of defense" when purchases over fifty dollars are made within a card user's state or within 100 miles of his residence.

6.11   Court: The Last Resort

Although self-help remedies are often valid alternatives to costly judicial process, your lawyer may offer the only practical recourse. Litigational approaches vary from state to state: You may proceed with a suit for money damages, a suit by confession on a promissory note, or a creditor's suit in a court of equity. After your day in court, supplementary proceedings can be instituted to collect on the judgment. These might include levying and executing on the debtor's property or garnishing his wages or bank account.

No lawsuit is pleasant, and a lawsuit against a customer, past or present, is especially distasteful. The costs of litigation—in time, in money, in heartache—can best serve to underscore the importance of developing a sound and comprehensive credit policy at the outset, one that is destined for the highest degree of success.

7 Listening to the Professionals

He who is always his own counsellor will often have a fool for his client.

—John Hunter

7.01 How the Professional Team Should Work

It's undeniable. From the very start you will need the help of the pros—the lawyer, the accountant, the banker, and the insurance broker or agent. The only thing open to question is how you will use them. The less enlightened might contend that the professional's proper role is curative—the lawyer's, to bring or defend a lawsuit; the accountant's, to prepare those tax returns by the 15th; the banker's, to satisfy a sudden need for cash; and the broker's or agent's, to provide the policy you need to land that big contract.

The truth is that a business owner's exclusive reliance on after-the-fact, emergency advice can only work to his detriment. A professional's best contributions are preventive, steering you clear of costly mistakes and toward opportunities that you might otherwise miss.

Working as a team, united by a common interest in the growth and prosperity of your business, your business counselors can offer you the widest range of relevant knowledge and experience available anywhere. Even when their opinions conflict—and they will—the interaction among your advisers, each with his own professional bias, will help you isolate the issues and weigh the pros and cons intelligently.

7.02   Making Good Use of Your Lawyer

Many small-business owners consult lawyers too seldom and too late. With the sheer volume and complexity of legal decisions you must face, your best bet is to consult your lawyer routinely. His input should prove indispensable in all of these areas:

> ▶ *Reviews.* As soon as he is retained, a good lawyer will check your past course of action—your corporate minute book, existing contracts, leases and insurance policies, other live documents—and make recommendations. Thereafter, he will made periodic legal checkups.
>
> ▶ *Counseling.* Your lawyer will offer guidance whenever you seek it, and will initiate ideas on his own.
>
> ▶ *Information.* Your lawyer can advise you in plain and simple English about the legality and efficacy of any action, and he should fill you in on the alternatives. What's more, it's his job to keep you abreast of changes in the laws that affect you and to alert you to the opportunities and pitfalls they carry.
>
> ▶ *Representation.* Of course, your lawyer will plead your case in court. Also count on him to represent your interests before government agencies, banks, other lawyers—anywhere he "speaks the language" better than you do.

What a Lawyer Is Supposed to Know
More specifically, here are a few areas in which any business lawyer who is worth his salt should be able to help:

> ▶ *Organization.* He will help you select the form of your business—corporation, partnership, or whatever—and see to the mechanics.
>
> ▶ *Buying, selling, contracting, and leasing.* Negotiating your best deal may become your lawyer's responsibility, and he can spot the tax issues too.
>
> ▶ *Financing and credit.* Your lawyer will shield you from the fine print in loan agreements and help you comply with all the new laws in this burgeoning area.
>
> ▶ *Taxes.* Your lawyer's eye will be toward the net dollar amount

on any transaction, and he will know how to maximize that amount even in light of the newest tax reform legislation.

▶ *Complying with federal, state, and local laws.* It is your lawyer's business to make you aware of the various pertinent laws and the easiest ways to conform to them.

▶ *Litigation.* Should a suit arise, or should you be forced to bring one, your lawyer (or his trial cocounsel) must be sharp enough and conversant enough with your business to tell your story to your best advantage.

The Quest for a Good Lawyer

Because of his uniquely diversified role, a lawyer can be critically important to your growth. Yet finding one who can make a difference in your business is a tough challenge. Forget about bar association referral services; they are helpful for individuals with consumer or domestic problems, but they cannot be selective enough for business clients. Also reject the advice of well-meaning friends who recommend their own lawyers; their needs are surely different from yours.

Watch out, too, for direct mail advertising. Although lawyers are allowed to advertise and to send descriptions of their experience and education by direct mail to you, they may not have the backgrounds that their materials claim. In fact, there have been an increasing number of instances in which people not admitted to the bar have held themselves out to the public as qualified professionals. Always verify the credentials of a lawyer through a bar association or by using reference sources that are available in most public libraries.

Other business owners in your general league are a good source of lawyer leads; their problems are apt to be similar to yours, and their success at solving them is worth your study. Nonlawyer professionals may also be helpful: They deal with business lawyers day in and day out and can probably spot a conscientious one; more important, they are privy to client comments, good and bad, and know who is satisfied with his lawyer and why. A final source of lawyer prospects are lawyers who are not seeking your account: house lawyers for local companies, government lawyers, and law school professors. These pros know other lawyers, and can judge competence using criteria such as the following:

- ▶ *Substantive knowledge.* Is the lawyer informed and up-to-date regarding major cases and legislation? Does he know the local procedures and practical considerations in the areas he covers? Are his legal research methods sound?
- ▶ *Fact-gathering ability.* Can the lawyer readily determine the level of factual research appropriate to each matter and the specific facts that are of key importance? Does he systematize the acquisition of the relevant facts?
- ▶ *Understanding problems.* Does the lawyer identify and address all the important aspects of his clients' problems? Does he focus on the core legal issues such as the terms of contracts, deeds, and other documents?
- ▶ *Communication with clients.* Does the lawyer explain issues, strategies for dealing with them, and procedural tactics clearly? Does he use appropriate means of communication, as promptly as necessary, to keep clients abreast of all developments, and does he mail copies of important legal documents?
- ▶ *Presence.* Does the lawyer use verbal skills, demeanor, suitable attire and appearance in order to maintain relationships with judges, juries, and other parties and their lawyers? Are there any factors that might impede or interfere with such relationships?
- ▶ *Writing ability.* Is the lawyer persuasive and clear in his writing? Is his writing concise and suited to the particular mode or matter involved?
- ▶ *Organization.* Does the lawyer organize his papers and files in a coherent manner? Does he anticipate deadlines, appointments, and other time factors through ticklers, schedules, and other functional reminder systems?
- ▶ *Negotiating judgment.* Does the lawyer prioritize goals in handling negotiations so that his concessions do not give away his clients' most important objectives? Does he have a sense for the timing of demands and concessions so that an opti-

mum, or nearly optimum, result can be gained within a reasonable time?

▶ *Allocation of time and resources.* Does the lawyer use time and resources in a way that maximizes the returns on these investments? Is he fair in balancing the needs of his clients for his own use of time, according to the relative importance of different client matters?

▶ *Ethics.* Does the lawyer have a good reputation for meeting professional responsibilities? Does he have a proper regard for the truth?

▶ *Staying within areas of competence.* Does the lawyer make appropriate referrals to other lawyers or other professionals when a matter is beyond his field of expertise? Does he obtain advice from experts, government agencies, or other suppliers of information whenever appropriate to his clients' needs?

▶ *Cooperativeness.* Does the lawyer cooperate with others so that he can derive their cooperation when needed? Are his employees, if any, satisfied with working conditions?

Once you have obtained a few recommendations regarding prospective lawyers, the work begins in earnest. Schedule an appointment with each prospect, even though you may have to pay for his time, and have a frank and full discussion. These are the things you will want to know about:

▶ *The size of his practice.* Even though a small firm can offer personalized attention, a large firm may have a broader range of expertise. Either way, satisfy yourself that the lawyer is not too busy to be accessible, and not so available that you can't help wondering why.

▶ *His client base.* Find out if representing other small-business owners is a major part of his practice.

▶ *His experience and specialty.* The lawyer's background should qualify him to advise you on routine matters as well as on major decisions.

▶ *His sounding board.* A cautious lawyer will consult other law-

yers, both generalists and specialists, for your benefit. Find
out whom he consults, and when.

▶ *His philosophy.* You won't learn everything in one interview,
but try to assess his basic attitudes toward the law and the
conduct of business. It is important that his views be compatible with yours so that you can feel comfortable in relying on
his judgment.

▶ *His style.* You will want a lawyer who can clearly, objectively,
and logically present both sides of an issue. Avoid the highly
opinionated, the pedantic, the overly glib, and the paternal-
istic.

▶ *His fee structure.* Minimum-fee schedules have been jetti-
soned, so you are left to informal comparisons and your own
judgment of what is reasonable. Fees are a big source of attor-
ney-client conflict, so discuss them openly at your first meeting.

What Price Advice?

You should consult with your attorney about the different ways
that legal services can be billed. Here are some of the fee options:

▶ A *retainer* is a periodic, fixed payment. What it buys can vary
tremendously from lawyer to lawyer. Sometimes a retainer will entitle a client to unlimited telephone and office consultations and
the review of routine documents. More often, a time limit is set,
and exceeding it will trigger an invoice. Depending on the partic-
ulars, retainers may or may not make economic sense for you, but
they will probably encourage freer use of your lawyer's time, and
that's good.

▶ An *hourly rate* is the most common, and often the fairest,
method of payment. Be sure to ask for advance estimates, and don't
be surprised if the hourly rate your lawyer quotes seems high: he's a
small-businessperson too, whose fees must support his entire overhead.

▶ Some routine matters may be charged at a *flat rate.* A simple
employment agreement or a corporate resolution, for example, usually bears a fixed charge.

► Collection cases and certain other matters can call for a *contingent fee*. Here, your lawyer is paid a negotiated percentage of any amount he recovers through settlement or at trial. He receives nothing if he recovers nothing. This is perhaps the only way a lawyer can be an entrepreneur within his own profession.

► Sometimes, a *bonus fee* beyond his regular billing is awarded the lawyer who wins an important case or issue, but only if it's been agreed upon in front.

A Client's Bill of Rights
This is the age of consumerism. Once you have hired the lawyer who seems to meet your standards, take advantage of all your rights as a client:

► *Confidentiality*. It is your right to have your secrets and confidences preserved by any lawyer you consult.
► *Full information*. You have a right to learn all you want to learn about any pending legal matter, and that knowledge should be communicated to you in language devoid of legalese. That means that your lawyer must keep you posted about his progress in every matter he's handling for you, and in litigation he must pass along all bona fide settlement offers as they are made. You also have a right to receive copies of any documents, correspondence, or pleadings prepared in your behalf.
► *Ultimate authority*. It is your problem-solving strategy that you will use, so you, not your lawyer, have a right to decide which legal methods and objectives to pursue and which to abandon. To this end, you have a right to hear all sides of the issue, both from your lawyer and from any other lawyer whose opinion you may solicit.
► *Reasonable fees*. As we have discussed, you and your lawyer will reach agreement on his fee structure, and that agreement will become a contract binding on both of you. Insist on reasonable fees set forth in frequent, itemized bills.
► *Competence*. You have a right to loyal, skillful, and energetic

representation by a lawyer who treats you courteously and considerately.

▶ *Termination.* If all does not go well, you have a right to call it quits upon payment of fair compensation for legal services properly performed. Your lawyer will be obligated to respect your confidences and deliver your files to your new lawyer.

Helping Yourself

For your ultimate good, you have one more right: the right to know what your lawyer expects of you. Hold up your side of the bargain, and nurture a relationship that will work to your absolute benefit. These are your obligations:

1. *Avoid "freebies."* Don't corner your lawyer on the golf course to discuss your latest problem. Human nature may force an off-the-cuff reaction that doesn't do you justice. Instead, treat legal matters as serious business, at your lawyer's office, on billable time, where together you can reach a deliberate, thoughtful solution.

2. *Don't seek easy answers.* Legal problems are often complex, so it is realistic to lower your sights and expect only competence, not miracles. Allow your lawyer the privilege of researching the law in depth and presenting the alternatives to you for discussion.

3. *"Tell the truth, the whole truth, and nothing but."* Don't withhold information, and don't slant it. And notify your lawyer about changes in your business as they occur; he will be the judge of whether they are relevant to your legal decision making.

4. *Finally, provide clear instructions.* Always let your lawyer know what you want him to do so that he has a reasonable chance of meeting your expectations.

7.03   Counting on Your Accountant

As discussed in Chapter 3, accounting is not a science but a descriptive art. It is not the mere application of a set of inflexible rules but the deliberate selection of choices that bears heavily on the very vitality of your business. For this reason, the accountant, like the lawyer, should not be brought into the decision-making process at the eleventh hour, but in the first. In recruiting your accountant, consider these criteria:

- *A good reputation.* Your accountant must be familiar with and sympathetic toward the needs of small business. He will provide data that will influence your most significant business decisions, so he must be totally trustworthy and scrupulously honest.
- *Experience and skill.* Of course, your accountant must be competent. Undoubtedly, the best accountant for you is one who really knows your type and size of operation and the ins and outs of its tax situation. The Certified Public Accountant (CPA) designation, given to an accountant who passes a qualifying state test, is itself an assurance of some knowledge and ability and is required before an accountant can "certify" (legally guarantee) a financial statement.
- *Time and interest.* Your accountant must learn all sorts of facts about your business in order to create the best accounting system for you. If he lacks the time or motivation, the finished product will instead be prepackaged and generalized, so look elsewhere.
- *Service.* Your accountant will be asked to set up a system to provide all the information you truly need, no more and no less. Be sure his range of services will meet your requirements.
- *Reasonable fees.* "Cheap" is often no bargain, and "expensive" is only too much if it is more than you would need to pay to have work of the same quality done by another accountant.

The Accountant's Work Product

Your accountant's role is multifaceted. These are among the services he may provide:

- *Systemization.* He will create your accounting system and maintain it.
- *Review.* Through audits, he will periodically review the func-

tioning of your system and recommend revisions in it as your business grows and changes.

► *Cost accounting.* He will trace profitability—and the lack of it—to nip profit drainers in the bud.

► *Inventory and budget analyses.* He will help you see the forest among all those trees.

► *Tax management.* He may not advocate clever, illegal tax-avoidance schemes, but he should initiate important tax-saving moves to (1) level peaks and valleys in the receipt of income, (2) accelerate or defer income and expense items, (3) divide income among related taxpayers, (4) build capital assets through legitimate depreciation, depletion, amortization, and other applicable deductions, (5) use all the deductions and exemptions available to you, and (6) save taxes through appropriate MACRS (section 3.07), fiscal-year (section 3.03), and other elections.

► *Assistance in raising capital.* He will prepare meaningful financial statements for prospective investors, banks, and other creditors, and may himself be a good source for money contacts.

Accounting Goals: Past, Present, and Future

The prime objective of accounting services is to provide information that you can understand and use in these three ways:

1. *Evaluating the past.* Accounting is history. Your accountant will study the hidden costs, tax liabilities, and unbalanced inventories that hurt you last year and the year before so that you can change your ways for the better in the year to come.

2. *Operating in the present.* Your accountant will provide the day-to-day financial facts you need to operate and control your business.

3. *Planning for the future.* Your accountant will chart the forecasts and projections that will form the basis of your future decisions, allowing you to budget your business resources with a minimum of waste and risk.

7.04   A Pro With Something to Sell—Your Banker

Your lawyer and accountant have nothing to sell but their independent judgment. That is not the case with your insurance agent or
broker, who peddles protection, or your banker, whose stock-in-
trade is cash. Nevertheless, for our purposes, the insurance man
(Chapter 8) and the banker are professionals. They are expert and
experienced business counselors who play an important role in the
success of virtually any venture.

It is usually not a banker that the businessperson selects, but the
bank where he works. Nevertheless, the banker's talent is tapped
on the same personal basis as any other professional.

You may choose your bank as you would any commercial (as
opposed to professional) firm to perform services for you, on valid
criteria such as these:

▶ *Services and location.* You may need a bank that offers specific
   services, such as payroll processing or a night depository. And
   if a bank is geographically convenient to you, so much the
   better.
▶ *Size.* You will want a bank big enough to fulfill your needs,
   now and in the future, yet not too big to take an interest in
   your growth.
▶ *Reputation.* Your bank can be a major source of business contacts, and therefore you will want to enjoy the benefit of your
   bank's good relations with others in the community and elsewhere.
▶ *General lending policy.* Loans are a bank's foremost product.
   You will want to know that the bank's lending policy will not
   exclude you, and, for example, whether it extends letters of
   credit to small-business owners, or short-term loans on accounts receivable or warehouse receipts.
▶ *Interest.* With the deregulation of banks, rates of interest paid
   on accounts may vary for competitive reasons. Although paying interest on corporate demand accounts may still be restricted, many banks offer automatic transfers of unused funds
   in demand accounts into interest-paying time or savings ac-

counts. If two banks are equally advantageous for other reasons, but one can generate more interest for your account, you might benefit from your interest in interest.

Banking on Your Bank

A bank must meet the same expectations you have for any professional. Its management philosophy, manifested in its attitudes and policies, must dovetail with your needs before a banker may be added to your professional team. Interview your banker just as you would any pro, and satisfy yourself on the following questions:

► *Is he interested in your business?* The bank that's on your side has declared itself in favor of the small business. And the banker for you is the one who is eager to grow with your business.

► *Is he familiar with your type of business?* A banker's knowledge of a business can go a long way toward offsetting his natural conservatism. And his experience and insight can prove to be valuable resources for you.

► *Is he progressive?* Without question, you will need a bank that extends credit to people in your position at a reasonable rate of interest. One test: If all the bank's assets are in readily liquidated securities, management is probably very conservative and tough on loans.

► *How much help is he willing to offer?* When a bank cannot lend you money, it should be able to find someone who can, such as a bank-owned Small Business Investment Company (SBIC) (section 12.03) or another venture capital source. A bank should also be willing to provide you with credit information on customers and suppliers, and it should want to make operating recommendations to help you grow successfully.

Cashing In

Once you have found a banker you can count on, start at once to build a productive relationship. The more he knows and cares about you, the more valuable he will become as a player on your professional team. And, wearing his money seller's hat, he will eventually be more receptive to a loan request.

Visit your banker frequently, and keep him fully and candidly informed about your business. He will be glad to receive all the hard information you care to share with him—annual financials, budgets, anything that helps tell your story. Demonstrate your confidence in the future, but acknowledge any business shortcomings too. Your banker, who may well know about any problems before you reveal them, will appreciate your honesty and astuteness, and he will welcome the opportunity to offer the advice that you just might need. What's more, you will be bolstering your banker's faith in your good character, a wise investment against the day you really need money.

Surprisingly, bankers are very reluctant to lend money to those who urgently need it. A strong, durable relationship with your banker can guard against an abrupt turndown. Whenever you're after a bank loan, adopt this bargaining posture:

1. *Come on like a winner.* The image you project is critically important. Everyone loves a winner. Hide any feelings of desperation, and act as if there is no doubt about your eligibility for a loan; the only purpose for your meeting is to agree on its terms.

2. *Back up your confidence with all the detailed data you can muster.* Bankers love facts and figures, so submit recent balance sheets, profit-and-loss statements, sales and profit projections (contemplating the use of loan proceeds and their payback), and personal financials. Put a ribbon on the package with positive research summaries and favorable publicity.

3. *Don't hide the negatives.* They'll be discovered, anyway. Lay all your cards out and, as best you can, explain the missing aces.

4. *Know what you want and shoot for it:*
   ▶ A *line of credit* is an open-end agreement by the bank to provide short-term credit up to a certain amount and under certain conditions. It is usually used for seasonal and discount purposes rather than for capital investment, and is a convenient way to firm up credit needs in advance.

▶ A *short-term loan* has a term of one year or less, and is also for working capital purposes, usually to take advantage of discounts. Some banks require a minimum deposit of 10 to 20 percent of the loan proceeds, effectively reducing available borrowed funds.

▶ An *intermediate-term loan* may be used for working-capital purposes too, or it may be an alternative to equity financing. Security or collateral may be real estate, securities, life insurance policies, equipment, accounts receivable, or warehouse receipts.

▶ A *long-term loan* is generally unavailable from a bank except for real estate financing.

▶ *Equity financing* is also not readily available from a bank, since bank investments are highly regulated. Many banks do own SBICs, and thus can provide access to venture capital; of course, banks do recommend investment opportunities to their select customers (see section 12.02).

5. *Negotiate for a loan as you would for anything else.* Ask for more than you need so that you can maintain a fallback position. Also, avoid off-the-cuff answers to hard questions; you can always defer to your lawyer, your partner, or your board, and can, with the benefit of time to plot a course, come back with a well-conceived counterattack.

6. *Don't be blinded by the appearance of success.* Getting a loan is not your purpose; getting the loan you need—with a reasonable interest rate, over a reasonable term, with only reasonable strings attached—is.

7.05 Teaming Up

The lawyer, the accountant, the insurance agent or broker, and the banker make up your professional team. Each must offer advice from his own vantage point, advice that may or may not be in harmony with that of the others. But each professional offers the access to the outside world upon which your business will feed.

8 Protecting Yourself

The winds and waves are always on the side of the ablest navigators.
                                                    —Edward Gibbon

8.01   Considering the Risks

Every business is exposed to obvious and not-so-obvious risks, risks that can cost big money and, at worst, can stymie future growth. Guard against those bleak possibilities by taking a conservative approach to protect your business as well as possible.

An affirmative risk-management program should be developed with the counsel of a competent insurance agent or broker, one familiar with your needs and the peculiarities of the insurance marketplace. Choose your agent carefully, as you would any professional, and count on him for these services:

- A thorough insurance-oriented evaluation of your current and proposed business operations
- A careful comparison of insurance alternatives
- Negotiation of contracts for coverage where your needs justify a special word on your behalf
- Administrative help in the establishment of simplified procedures within your business to handle necessary insurance paperwork
- Sound advice on loss prevention
- Guidance in your compliance with the Occupational Safety and Health Act (sections 9.06 and 9.07) and the Environmental Protection Act

► Assistance in claims processing
► An annual review of your insurance program

Every insurance agent will boast of access to financially stable in-surance companies that offer the least expensive coverage and the fastest claims service available anywhere. The truth is that brokers and agents are salespeople, and while most are reputable and sin-cere, all of them are looking to you and others like you to pay their rent. So buy your insurance cautiously from someone you know to be responsible and knowledgeable.

8.02   The Principal Principles

Finding a good insurance agent is only the beginning of your insur-ance planning. Granted, with its own jargon and its own legal rules, insurance is a bewildering concept for most laypeople, and most of us would rather leave insurance planning entirely to others. But sound business management demands your continuing control. With the aid of an agent you can trust, your decision making in insurance matters is bound to improve if you can get a firm grasp on a few basic principles:

► An *insurance policy* is simply a contract by which the insur-ance company or *carrier* undertakes the risk of paying out a dollar amount, or *benefit,* upon the occurrence of an unlikely event (usu-ally a casualty). In exchange, you agree to pay a fee, or *premium,* for the carrier's assumption of that risk. The policy describes what is covered, when, and to what extent, and your lawyer should study it carefully. It may also set out all kinds of procedures: how to file a claim, how to cancel coverage, how to assign your benefits, and even how to order more coverage.

► The evaluation of *risks* is essential to your loss prevention program and should focus on three areas as follows:
   1. *Property risks*—reflecting the exposure of your real and personal property, including both tangible and intangible

assets, to loss or casualty. A fire in your office or a theft of your vehicle are examples.

2. *Time risks*—reflecting the possibility of interruptions in your business or in your receipt of investment returns. Loss of sales during a communications breakdown is an increasingly common hazard for many businesses. If you lease out part of your office or plant building and a fire prevents your tenants from occupying their space, you may lose rental income unless you are insured.

3. *Liability risks*—involving your legal responsibilities to customers, business invitees, parties that use or rely on your products or services, and the public generally. Someone who slips on a floor on your premises because water or some other substance has been left there may have a right to legal recourse against you.

▶ The basic policy may be amended, or *endorsed,* at the outset or later on. Endorsements can be used to extend coverage to the particular risks of your business or locale, or they can be used to exclude unnecessary or separately insured perils, thereby lowering the premium. Special policies (on boilers or plate glass, for example) allow the deletion of such risks from general coverage, and thus they reduce insurance costs.

▶ Insurance policies can be *specific* or *blanket.* A specific policy identifies, or *schedules,* each item of insured property, locates it, and assigns a value to it. (Scheduling a valuable piece of equipment or an art object establishes its worth in front.) A blanket policy may offer greater flexibility in claims settlement by assigning value to insured property as a lot; a recovery limit is not set for any individual item, just for the aggregate.

▶ A *package policy* insures multiple risks in a single, comprehensive contract. When similar risks are packaged and insured together, lapping and overlapping coverage can successfully be avoided, and so can disputes between carriers. On the other hand, the packaging of dissimilar risks may deprive you of the broader coverage individual policies offer and will surely complicate your comparative analysis of competing policies.

► If there are wide fluctuations in the value of your inventory or other insurable assets, *reporting insurance* may be more economical for you. Unlike other insurance premiums, which are usually based on the value of insured property when purchased, reporting-insurance premiums and coverage can rise and fall with your periodic reports of asset holdings.

► The actual payout upon a loss can be the *actual cash value* (the cost less true physical depreciation) or *actual replacement cost.* These standards differ dramatically, so note which value the company elects in any policy you are reviewing. Spot whether an adjustment will be made in instances where insured items have a far greater value than their replacement costs; blueprints, manuscripts, microfilm, and computer software are good examples.

► The payout will be reduced if you fail to keep your part of the bargain described in a *coinsurance clause* (alias the *average clause,* the *percentage-of-value clause,* or the *contribution clause*). The coinsurance clause is used by carriers to keep insurance costs down by preventing selective underinsuring. It works like this: The insured agrees to buy coverage for, let's say, at least 80 percent of the value of his property. The payout is limited by the percentage of any deficit in coverage. An insured who is obliged to maintain 80 percent (or $80,000 coverage on $100,000 property), but who carries a policy of $40,000 only, will find his benefit cut in half at the time of loss. As property appreciates in value, the coinsurance clause calls for additional insurance purchases, so frequent reappraisals are a good idea.

► A *deductible*—the first dollars of loss, those that become your expense and not the carrier's—is a big premium saver. With a deductible, the benefits you buy can be limited to a percentage of a loss, can start at a specific dollar level, or can commence after the passage of a fixed loss-time period. A variation is the *disappearing deductible,* which gradually diminishes as a loss increases. For expected minilosses or really remote maxilosses, opt for the largest deductible you can reasonably afford, and your insurance costs should plummet.

8.03   An Insurance Strategy

As you start considering ways to handle your business risks, refer to this checklist:

1. Prepare an inventory of all your exposures.
2. Note which hazards can be reduced by precautionary measures, with estimates of the costs of such measures.
3. Determine whether specific or blanket insurance might protect you at a lower cost than your precautionary measures.
4. If the insurance cost is only slightly better than the cost of precautionary measures, consider whether the value of your time in processing insurance claims is likely to equal or exceed the marginal cost advantage for the insurance.

The partial listing of the insurance policies available to you (Exhibit 8-1) attests to the staggering complexity of insurance-purchasing decisions. Rely on an agent or broker who is more than a salesperson, and systematically evaluate your insurance needs. Follow these rules to avoid both underinsurance and overinsurance:

1. Pinpoint your legal liability—on contracts, leases, deliveries, and all other transactions—and consider covering your exposure.
2. Assess nontransactional risks too, such as any valuable artwork in your executive offices.
3. Evaluate your overall susceptibility to business interruptions, whether from a fire, a machine breakdown, the loss of a key employee or supplier, or in the transportation network that supports you.
4. Forecast your product liability to consumers, other users, and even nonusers. Remember that your implied and express warranties (section 5.02) may be ripe for insurance backup.
5. When you have translated all this vulnerability into a dollar projection, back off; only a tiny fraction of the risks your business faces is insurable. Your insurance professional will sort out what you can insure from what you cannot, including the biggest risk of all, the risk of plain old mismanagement.

Exhibit 8-1. Popular insurance products.

Accounts receivable insurance
Aircraft, owned, insurance
Automobile insurance
  liability, collision, comprehensive,
  medical payments, uninsured mo-
  torists' protection, and coverage
  on nonowned autos

Bailee's customers insurance
Blanket contractual coverage
Boiler insurance
Broad-form property-damage insur-
  ance
Business interruption insurance

Comprehensive general liability insurance
Credit insurance

Directors and officers insurance
Disability insurance
Dishonesty, disappearance, and de-
  struction coverage

Earthquake insurance
Employee's liability insurance

Fiduciary liability (ERISA)
Fire insurance, with extended coverage, special "all risk" extended
  coverage, and sprinkler damage
  coverage
Flood insurance
Forgery insurance

Inland transit insurance

Key-man life insurance

Leasehold insurance

Machinery equipment insurance
Marine transit insurance
Medical/dental/surgical insurance

Occupational disease coverage
Owner's, landlord's, and tenant's insurance

Parnership buy-sell funding
Payroll insurance
Plate glass insurance
Product liability insurance
Professional liability insurance
Profits and commissions coverage
Public liability insurance

Rent insurance

Salesperson's samples insurance
Security and theft insurance
  including robbery, safe, and alarm
  system insurance
Shareholder buy-sell funding
Sole proprietorship life insurance
Surety bonds for employees

Umbrella liability coverage

Valuable papers and documents insurance
Vandalism and malicious mischief
  coverage

Workers' compensation coverage

6. After you have learned what is insurable, forget all the inconsequential risks you really don't need to cover; insuring against predictable small losses is usually an expensive nuisance.
7. Finally, forget about insuring any risk you can deal with in some other way at less cost and effort. More on this cost-justification idea later, where self-insurance is considered (see section 8.08).
8. One footnote: Don't let your purchase of all the coverage you need and can afford conclude your insurance planning. Even for the insured, any loss is, at best, an inconvenience; at worst, a disaster. Loss prevention, with the guidance of a professional, is central to enlightened risk management.

8.04 Reading the "Fine Print"

All your well-intentioned insurance planning will prove ineffective if you take insurance at face value. Insurance companies exist to make money and, to that end, have earned a well-deserved reputation for "fine printing." With the help of your independent agent or broker, you can guard against hearing bad news like this, when it may be too late:

► *"You have no insurable interest."* Unless you would suffer a direct financial loss from the insured property's damage or destruction, don't ever expect a payout. A few policies even demand your sole and unconditional ownership before policy benefits attach. Be certain to inform the carrier of your ownership interest at the time of your insurance purchase and of any changes as they occur.
► *"You breached your warranty (or representation)."* Your application for coverage will elicit *warranties*, facts you guarantee to be true, and *representations*, assertions the carrier has a right to rely on. Any warranty or material representation that proves false may result in your policy being voided retroactively. So shun even a "white lie."

▶ *"The policy was never formally assigned to you."* Although accrued insurance proceeds are assignable without carrier permission, policies themselves cannot be assigned without the insurance company's consent. When buying insured property, make certain that contractual assignment provisions are fully observed; if not, obtain new coverage.

▶ *"The insurance company is not bound."* Where a standard insurance contract and its endorsement conflict, the endorsement governs. Your broker's opinion about a policy's true intent is not binding on anybody, so if there is ambiguity, obtain written clarification from the carrier. By the same token, your letter to a broker detailing changes in relevant facts or circumstances does not constitute legal notice to the carrier unless the broker happens to be an agent of the carrier. Insist on acknowledgment by the insurance company.

▶ *"You violated the policy."* Your violation of a policy term or condition usually suspends coverage until the violation is corrected. In a few states, however, coverage will remain suspended until specifically reinstated by the insurance company. Be safe: After any violation is remedied, ask for written confirmation that coverage has resumed.

▶ *"You have double coverage."* Buying a second policy on insured property requires the consent of the first carrier or endorsement for additional insurance on the first contract. Even if those requirements are met, you can never collect more than the value of the insured property; the two carriers on the book each pay a pro rata share of the loss.

▶ *"The loss is excluded."* Typical property policy exclusions include:

—Losses due to design deficiencies, error or omission, workmanship, materials, or specifications (however, unless collapse as a result of unknown causes is also excluded, a loss due to indeterminable cause is covered)

—Building collapse resulting from falling supports (an exclusion in most named peril policies—if wind or other named peril made the supports fall, the loss is covered)

—Losses due to war or nuclear attack (coverage against civil disorder can be obtained under a "federal crime" endorsement)

Transit policies often exclude acts of God, acts of criminals or public authorities, fault of shipper in packing the goods, and deterioration of perishable goods.

8.05 Protecting Your Property

Now let's look at your *property* insurance needs as your broker or agent might. Property coverage insures your business assets against all the risks you can think of, and then some.

▶ The basic *fire* policy is usually extended to cover direct damage from smoke, wind, hail, riots, aircraft, and most explosions. But don't feel too secure: Only stated risks are insured. You should consider endorsements to protect against *supplemental perils* (such as sprinkler damage, vandalism, and malicious mischief) and *climatic perils* (such as earthquakes and tornadoes). Also bear in mind that the loss of money and securities, and even the loss of business, is simply not considered in the standard fire policy.

▶ *Crime* policies may be necessary to the survival of your business. Where the risk of loss by crime is exceptionally high, you may turn to subsidized federal crime insurance. But whatever the source, consider *burglary* coverage, which affords protection against forced entries; *theft* coverage, covering disappearances without evidence of forced entry; and *robbery* coverage, insuring against losses by force, threats, or trickery on or off your premises. You can supplement these "external" crime coverages with "internal" insurance protection against *forgery*, and *fidelity bond* protection against employee dishonesty. Otherwise, package your crime insurance in a comprehensive *dishonesty, disappearance, and destruction* policy, and you will be safeguarded against employee thefts too.

▶ *Floater* and *transit* policies cover personal property against fire and casualty. Whereas a floater insures goods wherever they may be, a transit policy covers them only from a specific point of departure to a specific point of arrival.

A word about floaters: *Salespeople's samples* are excluded from automobile policies, so insure them separately. Also, goods you're holding for others deserve *bailee's customers* insurance.

To facilitate the valuation of property damaged in casualties, it is a good idea to keep a separate fact sheet on each building/addition/alteration and on units of fixtures and attached equipment, with original cost or acquisition prices and other information such as:

—The completion date of the respective construction, addition, or alteration; the acquisition dates of personal property items such as heating and air-conditioning apparatus

—The normal life expectancy

—The interior and exterior dimensions, with square footage of both areas

—The height of permanent floors, visual floors, permanent ceilings, and visual ceilings

—The construction materials used on exterior and interior walls, partitions, roofs, and foundations

—Makes, models, and serial numbers for all units of heating and for electrical, plumbing, air-conditioning, alarms, and other systems and fixtures

—Detailed descriptions of all other improvements, including composition materials, "R" factors for insulation materials, and other relevant information

—The amount of depreciation reserves accrued and tax deductions taken regarding all items of real and personal property through the valuation date, with specification of such date

▶ Remember your transit insurance needs too. *Inland transit* policies, including special parcel post insurance and rail transport insurance, can be limited or broad, and are often keyed to particular bill-of-lading forms. *Marine transit* coverage is usually sold on an all-risk, warehouse-to-warehouse basis and can be purchased at low cost by businesses complying with rigid packaging and shipping standards.

8.06   Don't Suffer the Consequences

Property coverage will compensate you only for the value of a damaged or destroyed asset. *Indirect and consequential* coverage, in all its forms, looks to the more far-reaching economic ramifications of property loss:

▶ If your business property is damaged or destroyed, *business interruption* insurance can restore your lost profits and reimburse you for ongoing operational and recovery expenses, even for the expenses of moving to temporary quarters. Your policy can be endorsed to protect you against so-called *contingent interruptions* such as a power failure or a business interruption suffered by a major supplier.

▶ *Rent* insurance covers the reduction or loss of income resulting from damage to rental property.

▶ *Leasehold* insurance covers the value of improvements to leased property when damage causes the cancellation of a lease.

▶ *Accounts receivable* insurance covers the cost of reconstructing damaged or destroyed receivable ledgers and supporting documentation; it is thus an alterative to maintaining duplicate records off premises. It can even compensate you for collections lost in the interim.

▶ *Credit* insurance may protect you against the contingency of customer bankruptcy. This coverage is designed to lessen the impact of an extraordinary insolvency. A high deductible meets or exceeds a reasonable allowance for usual bad debts. In the foreign marketplace, buy an *insolvency and political risk* policy from the Foreign Credit Insurance Association or the Import Export Bank.

▶ *Profits and commissions* coverage protects the commission of a seller whose income depends on a manufacturer's ability to supply a product.

▶ *Vehicle* coverages and endorsements usually include collision, comprehensive losses, and towing charges, as well as driver liability.

8.07 Do Unto Others . . .

Liability insurance protects your business against the claims of others who sustain personal injury or property damage for which you are legally responsible. Courts are continually enlarging the scope of your legal liability to others, and damage awards relentlessly grow larger year by year. Apart from a comprehensive *general liability* policy, specialized policies may be important.

▶ *Workers' compensation* and *occupational disease* coverage, possibly mandatory in your state, will cover your liability to employees for job-related injuries or diseases—liability that is yours even though you may not be negligent. Those employees who are permissively excluded from coverage can be protected under *employer's liability* insurance. Both worker's compensation and employer's liability should be carefully integrated with *disability* insurance (to reimburse an employee's salary or part of it when workers' compensation benefits do not apply) and with any disability provisions in your retirement plan.

▶ *No-fault* auto insurance plans are progressively redefining needs in the critical auto liability area. Such plans prescribe immediate payments to passengers in insured vehicles for lost wages and actual expenses, without regard to fault; pain and suffering damages are limited by statute. Where no-fault has not yet been enacted, *auto liability* coverage is often required by law, and is always a necessity.

You are protected if your business vehicle causes an accident resulting in personal injury or property damage. The most your insurer will pay for damages resulting from any one accident is the "liability insurance limit" shown on the face of your policy—the limit applies no matter how many persons and autos are involved and regardless of the number or magnitude of claims made against you. Tort law may hold a business liable for auto accidents caused by its employees, even when they're driving leased vehicles or their own vehicles, so buy *nonowned auto* coverage and contractually bind your employees to maintain adequate coverage on their own cars.

While premium costs can be lowered by opting for the highest possible deductibles, most insurers are prohibited by law from providing deductibles for bodily injury; or else, they refuse to allow those deductibles so that they can control the entire handling of personal injury cases. Coverages other than liability include:

1. *Collision* protection, which pays for damage to your vehicles less the amount of your deductible
2. *Comprehensive* coverage, which guards against noncollision casualties such as fire, theft, and vandalism, on a deductible or actual cash-value basis
3. Medical payments for passengers of your vehicles
4. *Uninsured motorist's* protection, which insures the passengers of your vehicles against injury caused by a driver without liability coverage

▶ *Product liability* coverage is costly and increasingly hard to get, but it's indispensable to many businesses. Courts in all the states have adopted the view that an individual who is injured because of a defective product or inadequate warning of a known, substantial, but not obvious hazard as to a product, can recover from the manufacturer or marketer of such product, even if no negligence can be proved (see discussion of the "strict liability" rule in section 5.02). Although consumer products such as power mowers and hand tools are often involved in claims and litigation over alleged defects and defective warnings, machinery and equipment used in manufacturing and business, such as lift trucks and metal working tools, may trigger even greater liabilities.

Juries have been persuaded to award increasingly large recoveries in the cases that are not settled, in part perhaps as a reaction to the increase in the size of the defendant corporations. Sometimes internal company documents reveal that the company knew of particular dangers but decided to save production costs by not adding relatively inexpensive precautionary devices. The manufacturer is deemed an expert, and he, not the injured user, is thought to be in the best position to bear the risk of accidental injury. Where a marketer is sued because of uncertainty as to manufacture, the strict liability theory has been applied if the seller or a distributor, wholesaler or retailer, turned over a packaged product that was uninspected or subject to recall notice or other notice of hazardous condition or to inadequate warning labels.

Product liability judgments running into the millions of dollars are no longer a rarity. Manville Corporation, which had been one of the thirty corporations used for the Dow Jones Industrial Stock Index, deliberately elected bankruptcy as a means to limit its exposure to asbestos-related product liability claims. Most people have also heard about the enormous numbers of claims triggered by the Audi 5000 (an acceleration problem) and the Firestone 500 (sudden deceleration/tire failure). The root problem is older, however: When the Ringling Brothers Barnum & Bailey Circus elected in 1942 in favor of a cheaper, less flame-retardant canvas for its big top, the survivors of a resulting infamous fire took over the company's entire profits for twenty years ("infamous" in part since, in addition to hundreds of deaths, there was no publicity because of a national policy to suppress news stories that might be demoralizing during the wartime victory effort). While the review of the cases in this area is more than a little depressing, it is encouraging that product liability insurance is still available from some insurance carriers, even though the price may be a little steep. With many insurers withdrawing from this type of coverage, placing this type of policy may be difficult; yet, such a policy is more indispensable than ever if you manufacture or distribute products having average or above-average risks of bodily injury.

▶ *Umbrella liability* coverage insures excess claims over and above the limits of other liability policies, including your general liability policy. Intended to cover only extraordinary claims, umbrella coverage is usually written with a large deductible and lets you purchase your other liability policies at lesser limits with smaller premiums.

8.08   Self-Insurance: Doing It Yourself

With so much expense and sometimes so little to show for it, more and more businesses are deciding to bear the risk of certain kinds of loss internally. The concept is neither novel nor outlandish: Deductibles and uninsured risks in "named peril" policies always create self-insurance exposure for businesses.

Risk retention should never be a negligent default in planning. It can be a deliberate and positive way of reducing overall costs and enhancing cash flow when losses are predictable or when insurance costs are prohibitively high.

Self-insurance must be a rational program geared to your enterprise's fiscal condition, and not a simpleminded jump at front-end cost savings. Some businesses limit their self-insurance exposure to 5 percent or less of their net working capital; others set a maximum of one percent of average pretax earnings over the last five years. Your attorney can work with your accountant to develop a conservative risk profile for your enterprise.

In general, any good self-insurance program is a product of the kinds of risks that are retained. Small property damage exposure, for instance, probably needs little or no formal structuring: As losses occur, they are merely charged against an operating budget. If a business has the working capital and management orientation to retain major risks, it will ordinarily set up a loss reserve, either on paper or actually funded, with the premium that otherwise would be used to pay an insurer. If the retained risk is a deductible, the loss reserve amounts to the difference between the cost of coverage from the first dollar and the premium actually paid.

As a self-insurer, you should eventually try to accumulate at least twice as much as you might lose in a single occurrence. In the meantime, prepare to finance your retained risk by making a one-time, start-up contribution by slowing your phasing into self-insurance until the fund can hold its own or by arranging standby bank loans capable of a quick drawdown at current interest rates.

Although your reserve might be an expensive undertaking (especially since it may be ineligible for tax deductions except when losses are incurred), it can become a source of income through investment rather than an insurance-premium drain. And loss control may well be improved; when each profit center bears the risk of its own losses, managers will diligently strengthen their safety and security precautions.

One way to start retaining risks is to opt for large-scale deductibles where straight dollar amounts are excluded from each loss payout. The amount of retained loss can be fixed, and the balance can be insured with carriers offering claims management and loss control services.

Another way to combine self-insurance with classical policy purchases is *retrospective rating*. Retrospective rating is popular in general liability and in auto and workers' compensation lines (where allowed by law), and it is particularly useful where a business anticipates a marked improvement in its claims experience.

Retrospective rating works this way: You pay your insurer a basic premium to approximate the cost of administering your program, including the adjustment of your claims. You also pay an *excess loss* (catastrophe) premium to buy insurance on claims over a predetermined self-insurance limit. The total of actual losses for a one-year term is multiplied by a *loss-conversion factor* to establish the insurer's actual fee for handling claims.

Retrospective rating is one innovative way of fixing an income floor for the insurer and an expense ceiling for the insured. Risk retention, whether through retrospective rating or any of a stunning variety of other imaginative approaches, is surely not desirable for every business; legal, inspection, and administrative expenses alone will restrict some to traditional insuring. Yet everyone should have an open mind to the dynamic opportunities of insurance. With the aid of a top-notch insurance adviser—and, of course, your attorney—relate your risk-management needs to the financial position and objectives of your business.

9 Relating to the Rank and File

If thou art a master, sometimes be blind; if a servant, sometimes be deaf.

—Thomas Fuller

9.01   Your Goals and Theirs

Good employer relations do not spring like a phoenix from the ashes of a union organizer's cigar; they grow over time in businesses that adopt personnel policies that are sound, employee directed, yet cost-effective. Maintaining high standards in the following areas will pay off in terms of a stable, remunerative work force:

▶ *Security.* Be neither arbitrary nor discriminatory in hiring, firing, and promoting. And underscore your concern with a solid health-and-welfare program.
▶ *Fairness.* Create a merit system based on objective job evaluations, and offer dedicated employees (1) the income they need to maintain their standard of living, (2) a reasonable opportunity to build their net worth, (3) a cushion against any catastrophe that might befall them, (4) an allowance for their retirement, and (5) a hedge against inflation. Also, encourage your employees to voice their real complaints.
▶ *Good working conditions.* Physically, this means a safe and decent place to work. Psychologically, it means a supportive environment of acceptance, dignity, and respect.
▶ *Humanity.* Your strong interest in your employees' well-being will inspire them. And the sense of participatory responsibil-

ity and accomplishment you instill in them will mature into a loyalty that's all to your benefit.

▶ *Certain written understandings.* While employment contracts are not generally advisable, there are three situations that call for written agreements:

1. If the employee is expected to maintain the confidentiality of proprietary information such as trade secrets used in the business
2. If the employee will be doing work that may involve the development of inventions or discoveries that should, by reason of its subsidization, be covered by assignments to the business (see section 4.06)
3. If you cannot obtain the services of a key person without giving him an employment agreement (you may wish to consult the checklist set forth in Exhibit 9-1)

9.02 Federal Law

The nondiscriminatory business objectives described in section 9.01 have a statutory basis. Equal employment opportunity, for example, is guaranteed by Title VII of the 1964 Civil Rights Act (Title VII). The Act prohibits discrimination on the basis of race, creed, color, sex, or national origin by all employers of fifteen or more persons and by all educational institutions, employment agencies, state and local governments, and labor-management committees for training. Other laws have expanded Title VII's scope to cover handicapped persons and veterans and enlarged the enforcement powers of both the federal and state governments:

▶ The Equal Employment Opportunity (EEO) Act gives the Equal Employment Opportunity Commission (EEOC) power to sue for the kinds of discrimination outlawed by Title VII.

▶ The Equal Pay Act, a part of the Fair Labor Standards Act, demands equal pay to men and women for equal work.

▶ The Age Discrimination Act prohibits discrimination on the basis of age, particularly benefiting those between ages 40 and 70.

Exhibit 9-1. Checklist for employment agreement.

☐ **Term.** The duration of the agreed employment relationship can be negotiated, but usually an employer will seek to have rights to terminate at any time for cause and, in any event, upon the sale, merger, or discontinuance of the business.

☐ **Compensation.** The components of the agreed pay package may include salary, bonus, or incentive compensation; the fringe benefits to which other employees are entitled; and possibly special vacation, company car, stock options, or other provisions. Particular care is needed if a bonus is based on "net profit," since the provision for such a bonus will reduce the amount of profit otherwise computed.

☐ **Duties.** The employee's basic duties should be described. The employer should reserve rights to assign services or other functions to be performed, the hours of the day or night when performance is to be rendered, and the manner of the performance.

☐ **Loyalty and due care.** Acting with a conflict between personal interest and that of the company should be restricted, as well as unlawful or negligent acts or omissions, possibly with standards of "best efforts" or "good faith" if the likelihood of mistakes through human error is significant.

☐ **Confidentiality, trade secrets, and inventions.** The protection of trade secrets, customer lists, and confidential information may be so essential to your business that you should address these matters in a totally separate agreement—many companies use employee agreements that cover these subjects only. Restrictions on copying or removing company records, files, and documents are important, as are assignments to the employer of rights to inventions and of writings developed in the course of employment. Injunctive relief, as well as legal damages, should be stipulated for breach of any of these provisions.

☐ **Restrictive covenant.** Although most employers would like to prohibit any kind of competition not only during employment but for all eternity after an employee departs, the law and the courts require that any restrictions in this area be reasonable in time and geographic application and not limit the use of general skills gained in a business career. Some jurisdictions do not enforce restrictive covenants. Others hold that competition cannot be restricted, but only unfair competition. As the law in your area may differ from that in other states, you will need specific legal advice in preparing the language for your agreement. Your attorney will probably encourage you to set out a short time period and a small geographic area in which competition will be restricted in order to make the agreement more likely to be enforced should a breach occur. It is also advisable in general to define which businesses are to be considered competitive with your business within the meaning of your employee's covenant.

(continued)

Exhibit 9-1. *Continued*

☐ **Affiliates.** If you have more than one company or entity doing business, you should refer to the affiliated concerns in various parts of the agreement, and particularly in the restrictive covenant. Usually, the term "affiliates" is defined as being those enterprises, incorporated or unincorporated, of which at least 50 percent of the equity is owned by the same person or persons owning at least 50 percent of the equity of the employer company.

☐ **Notices.** The agreement should specify that no advance notice is required in the event the employee is terminated for cause. In general, notices should be sent to the addresses of the parties as set forth in the agreement, with copy to the employer's attorney.

☐ **Legal counsel.** If the employee is not represented by legal counsel and you are, there should be a recital acknowledging that the employee decided not to be so represented.

☐ **Governing law, arbitration, and miscellaneous.** It is usually advisable to spec-ify the state whose law governs the contract, an agreement to submit disputes to arbitration, a restriction on assignment of the agreement, a requirement that modifications be in writing, a statement that if any provision is not valid, the other provisions shall remain in full force and effect, a statement that there are no understandings other than those set forth in the agreement, and a provision for attorney fees and legal costs to be awarded to the party prevailing in any dispute under the agreement.

▶ The National Labor Relations Act bans both internal and external discrimination by unions, and it prohibits employers from discriminating on the basis of union membership or nonmembership.

▶ Finally, some state laws set even higher standards than these federal laws do, with most of these laws, outside the southern states, applying to companies that have fewer than fifteen employees—in some states, as few as three employees will bring the nondiscrimination laws into play.

9.03   Equal Employment Opportunity

Title VII and the EEO amendments prohibit discrimination in hir-ing and firing and in promotions, privileges, compensation, and conditions of employment. If you have not discriminated in the past and are not a government contractor, however, you will not be required to adopt an affirmative action program to employ and promote members of minority groups. You can obtain various EEOC guidelines from the Superintendent of Documents, U.S. Government Printing Office, Washington, D.C. 40402, including "Uniform Employee Selection Guidelines," "Guidelines on Sexual Harassment," "Guidelines on National Origin," and "Guidelines on Religious Discrimination."

There are exceptions to the prohibitions of discrimination relating to "bona fide occupational qualifications," but the application of these exceptions is rare indeed. Watch out for these compliance pitfalls:

1. Don't advertise for a "girl Friday" (that's sexist) or a "recent college grad" (that's age discriminatory, or possibly arbitrary as to the college degree, or both).

2. Avoid lie detector tests or other third-degree tactics on employment applications. Even seemingly harmless informational questions have been held discriminatory by the EEOC. Asking an applicant's place of birth, hair or eye color, and even height and weight are challengeable as discriminatory by race or national origin.

An inquiry about marital status can be discriminatory, and asking a person's age is not permitted unless the application form acknowledges that discrimination on the basis of age is illegal.

Bringing an applicant's educational background into question can constitute a violation too. Requiring a high school diploma, for example, has been held as discrimination against minorities in employment situations where graduation need not rationally be a requirement for a specific job.

Even credit ratings and arrest records (but not conviction records) are improper areas of inquiry; they have been held to discriminate unfairly against minorities.

3. Try to eliminate subjective evaluations throughout the hiring process. Coworker preference and traditional role stereotypes are totally unacceptable recruitment criteria.

4. It may be best to omit employment and promotion testing altogether. So many tests have been held discriminatory against undereducated and foreign-born minorities that their validity and legality are highly doubtful. Any tests you do adopt should first be validated as both job related and nondiscriminatory.

5. Do not limit fringe benefits to "heads of household" or "principal wage earners"; it's illegal. So is excluding husbands in cases where wives are benefited. Pregnancy and childbirth must be treated as any other temporary disability. The additional cost of providing these benefits to women is no defense for their omission.

Discrimination on account of pregnancy is equivalent to discrimination on account of sex, so you can't discharge an employee because of her pregnancy or require her to take an unpaid leave of absence before her doctor says she should not work. If you have a short-term disability plan that ensures paid leaves for those who break legs or are otherwise temporarily disabled, then a pregnancy leave with pay is also required.

6. Never fire anyone without giving him the courtesy of an exit interview where he can learn the specific reasons for your decision. Be specific: Personnel file notations such as "he can't get along with coworkers" or "she received an adverse supervisor report" have given rise to covert discrimination charges.

9.04 The EEOC and You

Title VII and the EEO amendments are enforced by the EEOC, and its enforcement powers are considerable. Government contractors and employers of over 100 employees are automatically monitored by the Commission, since the EEOC is obliged to file periodic informational reports. Other employers subject to the EEO (mainly businesses with fifteen or more employees) are scrutinized only after a complaint is filed by anyone with 180 days of an alleged violation.

Upon receiving a complaint, the EEOC will send a copy of it along with form interrogatories to the respondent-employer. The employer's answers to interrogatories, prepared under a lawyer's direction, may be the only input the Commission will consider on its behalf. The answers must demonstrate both nondiscriminatory intent and nondiscriminatory results—an uphill challenge, at best.

Should the EEOC find reasonable cause for the complaint, a conciliation agreement may be consummated: The employer may promise to cease from engaging in the questionable practice; the employer may agree to appropriate affirmative action to correct its discriminatory course; or the employer may agree to hire (or rehire) the aggrieved applicant (or employee), with or without back pay. Failure to reach agreement can result in the Commission's issuance of a "right to sue" letter, entitling the complainant to file a civil suit against the employer within ninety days. Title VII is remedial, not punitive, yet its muscle can devastate the violating employer. Courts can award up to two years of back pay to huge groups of women or minority employees. In addition, affirmative action remedies may be awarded, setting precise and expensive timetables for hiring minorities and upgrading goals.

One very strong recommendation: Initiate your own affirmative action program; then a court will never need to do it for you. Voluntary affirmative action programs are the best defense against any eventual equal employment opportunity complaint, and they serve to make key personnel sensitive to the law's requirements. What's more, by executive order, all government contractors are required to undertake affirmative action programs, reflecting special consideration for Vietnam veterans and the handicapped.

9.05 Two Acts to Follow

The Equal Pay Act applies to employers of two or more persons, other than an owner or family members, and requires that pay be determined only on the basis of skill (the experience, training, education, and ability required for the job), the effort actually expended on the job, and responsibility.

The Age Discrimination Act applies to employers of twenty or more persons. The Act allows discrimination on the basis of age only when there is a "bona fide occupational qualification" (as there might be for an acting or modeling job), and permits the imposition of physical fitness standards only if they are not linked directly to age. Although some benefits may reasonably diminish with age, pursuant to a legitimate employee benefit plan (for example, the same life insurance dollars can be used to buy a smaller policy for an older worker), there are three important limitations on policies concerning older employees:

1. Employees over age 65 must continue to be covered by the same group health arrangements provided to younger employees.
2. Involuntary retirement before age 70 is prohibited.
3. An employer may not reject an older job applicant merely because his employment might be more costly.

Both acts are enforced by the U.S. Department of Labor. Its Wage and Hour arm randomly surveys employers in interstate commerce and investigates complaints from all sources. Much like the Equal Employment Opportunity Commission, the Labor Department negotiates settlements when it finds that violations have occurred. If you have made a settlement, you will be well advised to demand written releases from further action; otherwise, you may be subject to later litigation for back pay and other damages.

Remember to include the requirements of the Equal Pay Act and Age Discrimination Act in your voluntary affirmative action program.

9.06   What is OSHA?

Another broad employee-protective federal statute, the Occupational Safety and Health Act (OSHA), covers virtually all employers except those whose health and safety standards are regulated by other laws. OSHA defines your general duty "to furnish a place of employment free from recognized hazards causing or likely to cause death or serious physical harm." A "recognized" hazard has judicially been interpreted as one that is preventable and generally known within an industry or to the public at large. Although the hazard must be identifiable, it need not be obvious; airborne particles that can only be detected by delicate sensors are a recognized hazard.

OSHA makes it unlawful to terminate or discipline an employee who refuses to do work that the employee reasonably believes exposes him to immediate and substantial risk of bodily injury. Discrimination against an employee who has complained to OSHA and filing false information with OSHA are also prohibited.

OSHA has been amended to provide some relief to small businesses having ten or fewer employees. Concerns of this size are exempted from the OSHA record-keeping requirements, and, if you have not had a problem evidenced by either an employee's complaint or an accident that resulted in death, then OSHA inspectors will not attempt to visit your plant or office. Your local OSHA office will advise you about whether you qualify for these or any later-adopted statutory exemptions.

Beyond the general employer duties just referred to, the Occupational Safety and Health Administration (also referred to as OSHA), a part of the Department of Labor, has promulgated specific industry standards. These are derived from data gathered by the Bureau of Statistics and from the continuing research conducted by the National Institute of Occupational Safety and Health. Contact your local OSHA office for free copies of "The Target Health Hazards," "General Industry OSHA Safety and Health Standards Digest," and "Construction Industry OSHA Safety and Health Standards Digest." At the same time, for financial and other guides, request the "OSHA Handbook for Small Businesses" and, to help meet your reporting requirements, "Recordkeeping Requirements Under the Occupational Safety and Health Act of 1970."

Take advantage of the educational and training programs OSHA has spawned. The National Safety Council has developed courses in compliance procedure, which are presented nationwide. Aided by private and public sponsors, some employers have been encouraged to set up their own programs in employee safety, in first aid, and in the assessment of working conditions. These voluntary steps are sensible—they are good morale boosters, they aid in

OSHA compliance, and, in the long run, they maximize business productivity.

9.07   Doing Battle

In the years to come, OSHA will truly become a joint federal-state responsibility. As more and more states pass OSHA laws and build enforcement machinery, state agencies will assume a greater share of the inspection and adjudication functions. Right now, though, OSHA is largely a federal program.

Although the law has authorized OSHA inspectors to enter an employer's premises without any warrant or notice, the Supreme Court has held that either a warrant or permission of the owner is required for such visits. Often, when OSHA inspectors went to court to obtain such warrants, the judge found that there was no probable cause for believing that a violation of the law was occurring. Other judges, however, have found that probable cause does exist on the basis of information and belief, and have issued the search warrants as requested.

If an OSHA inspector arrives at your place of business and asks for permission to enter, you may want to ask for time to consult with your attorney. If the inspector then says that a serious employee complaint is involved and that a warrant will be obtained, you may decide to offer to advise the inspector within twenty-four hours about whether permission will make a warrant unnecessary so that he will not have to go to court. It should not be necessary to make an immediate decision. Remember, most OSHA violations only result in fines amounting to a few hundred dollars.

An inspection usually starts with a request to see your OSHA records. You will be advised of your legal rights, and the inspector will ask that a representative of your employees be present during the inspection. You or a management representative should also plan to be present, and if air or noise pollution levels are high, you should invest in your own measuring equipment and take measurements at the same time the inspector takes his. If any employees have been injured by machinery, you can expect that machine guards will be a focus point for the inspection. In air pollution cases, the inspectors may assume that employees forget or refuse to wear respirators or other personal protective gear; in other words, it may be presumed that you should be reducing these hazards through environmental engineering rather than passing the buck to your employees. If potent chemicals are used in your operations, you should be doing business only with extensive input from your lawyers and chemical experts.

If any OSHA violations are found upon the inspection, you will be notified in writing of each specific violation and the time period fixed for its correction (the *abatement period*). Such *citation notices* must be posted for all employees to see. A *notice of proposed penalty* may accompany the citation; the amount of the penalty will be determined by the size of your business, the gravity of the violation, your good faith, and your history of previous violations. If the violation is not corrected within the abatement period, a *noncompliance notice* will be issued and a substantial, additional penalty may be assessed on a daily basis.

A citation or penalty can be contested by notifying OSHA in writing of your intention to contest within fifteen days after receiving a notice of proposed penalty. Then, you and your lawyer can contest any or all these elements:

- ▶ *The citation.* You might contend that your mode of operation is just as safe as the standard and request a permanent variance.
- ▶ *The abatement period.* You can request an extension of time—or a temporary variance—by showing good reason for not complying within the allotted time.
- ▶ *The proposed penalty.* You can challenge the amount of the penalty in light of the small size of your business, the relative insignificance of the violation, your good intentions, and your clean record.

After you notify OSHA of your intent to contest, the matter will be docketed for a hearing before the OSHA Review Commission, an independent federal agency with courtlike trial procedures in force. Barring a last-minute agreement with the Administration, you will be granted your day in court.

9.08 What About Unions?

Even though management and labor depend on each other for their very survival, they are normally in a state of conflict. You and your co-owners (along with the high-level executives you recruit) are dedicated to effecting cost economies wherever you can, and, as owners of capital, you may claim both the right and the obligation to decide how best to use that capital. Your rank-and-file employees, on the other hand, are striving for the best compensation package and working conditions they can, and, since their jobs may be lost to business reverses, they may feel that they are entitled to have some influence on decisions. Generally speaking, no one employee can usurp managerial authority, but a united organization of employees can effectively bargain with employers to gain a major role in business decision making.

Employers have traditionally resisted attempts to unionize as threats to their right to manage and as assaults on their pocketbooks. Your reaction to the preliminary steps taken by your employees will make all the difference in your long-term employee relations and in the ongoing productivity and profitability of your business.

Your Union Strategy

Before a union representative pays you a visit, he will probably have gathered the signatures of at least 30 percent of the employees in the proposed "bargaining unit." They will have given authorization for the union to petition the National Labor Relations Board (NLRB or Board) for an election by secret ballot if you refuse to recognize the union. (A 30 percent response is a sufficient show of interest to support a petition; a 50 percent response may allow union recognition even without an election.)

With authorizations in hand, the representative will inform you of his success. Keep the encounter brief and civil. Listen to any demands, and let the representative know that you may discuss them with your lawyer before making a commitment.

If you and your lawyer have any reasonable doubt that the union is the collective bargaining choice of a majority of the workers in a legally organizable bargaining unit, he will draft a refusal to recognize the union. Although your refusal to recognize a union that legitimately represents a majority can lead to later charges of unfair labor practices, recognizing a union that does not represent the majority is also illegal. When in doubt, opt for the refusal and let the NLRB conduct a secret election to determine the union's true status.

Once the union representative files the petition, you will receive an NLRB questionnaire seeking to learn whether your operation meets the Board's self-imposed jurisdictional standards. If it does, you may request a hearing to test whether or not the voting unit (those workers who will be eligible to vote) is a true bargaining unit over which the Board should maintain jurisdiction. Finally, if all is in order, an election agreement will be signed, explicitly defining the bargaining unit and setting the election date.

On the Campaign Trail

During the thirty days or so between the execution of the election agreement and the balloting, you may conduct a "soft-sell" antiunion campaign. It should be both thoughtful and deliberate. Be careful to avoid any unfair tactics; improper conduct can induce the NLRB to set aside a management victory; and your repeated violations of the National Labor Relations Act can force union recognition even without an election. So, conduct an issues-oriented campaign under your lawyer's guidance, and concentrate on these points:

1. Play up all the benefits your employees enjoy; they may not understand them fully.
2. Cite the advantage of dealing with you on a personal, one-to-one basis, rather than with a large, impersonal union with its own rules and regulations.
3. Compare your employees' wages and benefits with your com-

petitors' programs. If you have been more generous, drive that fact home; if you haven't been, explain why. No union can win more for its members than an employer can afford to pay.

4. Review the costs and other disadvantages of unionization. Your employees should be told about "one-man rule" (union bossism) if it applies, or seniority systems that penalize younger, ambitious workers.

5. Point out that the ballot is secret and that signing an authorization does not bind an employee to vote for union representation. Hasten to add, however, that the majority will decide and that its decision will not be held against any employee.

6. Describe how difficult it is to remove a union if it is later decided not to have been worth the effort and expense.

7. Let your employees know that they are not obligated to speak with the union representative, and urge them to report any threats or coercion.

8. Correct any rumors, misrepresentations, or distortions of fact with clear rebuttals. First, quote the union's allegation verbatim, and then tell the truth. Your credibility should zoom.

Telling Your Story

But how do you get the word out? In each case, your message should be simple, straightforward, and personal and should be carefully reviewed by your lawyer. These methods of communication are most successful:

- ▶ *Letters.* Personal letters sent to employees' homes are always very effective. A final letter rebutting the union's principal charges can be mailed just before the election.
- ▶ *Notes in pay envelopes.* This is a good way to relate union costs to take-home pay.
- ▶ *Handbills.* If distribution by the union is prohibited in certain work areas, voluntarily impose the same restriction on yourself.
- ▶ *Films.* Some popular antiunion films have been held "inflam-

matory" and thus unfair, so get your lawyer's OK before showing any movie.

▶ *Speeches.* Speeches are perhaps the most effective way to
communicate with your employees, but they must not be
coercive; nor may they be delivered within twenty-four hours
of the election.

Keeping It Clean

Union elections must be free and open. Unfair campaign tactics
are prohibited. Here are a few examples of what you may not do—
behavior held to be unfair:

▶ You may not poll employees about their sympathies, but do
listen to any unsolicited information your employees voluntarily offer.

▶ You may not threaten or imply a loss of jobs or benefits (or,
for that matter, predict the company's failure) after a union
victory. Nor may you promise extraordinary wage increases or
other benefits after a union defeat.

▶ In the broadest sense, you may not spy. No management personnel should ever attend a union meeting, and no employer
representative may be present in the voting area during the
election.

▶ Once an election agreement has been signed, you may not
withhold employees' names and addresses from the union or-
ganizers.

▶ You may not visit employees at their homes to talk against the
union.

▶ Although you may establish reasonable rules about solicitation and the distribution of materials in work areas and on
company time, you must apply them fairly and uniformly to
union and management alike; any restriction must be clearly
posted for all to see.

▶ You may neither favor antiunion employees nor discriminate
against prounion employers. To avoid discrimination charges,
your lawyer may advise you to fire no one during the campaign.

▶ While you may not be dispassionate, you may not issue statements that are untrue, misrepresentative, or, foggiest of all,
"inflammatory."

The Election and Its Aftermath

The NLRB will do its best to ensure that both the campaign and
the election are carried out democratically and by its rules. The
election will be conducted by a Board agent, with one observer
present from each side. Yet the outcome may not be the final word.

If you are successful, the union may attempt a reversal in one of
three ways.

1. Because it is illegal to refuse to recognize a union unless you
   genuinely believe it does not represent the majority, the
   union may contend that it had sufficient authorizations before the election and that your "refusal to bargain" at that
   time should force recognition now.
2. The union may charge you with unfair labor practices, entitling it to a new election.
3. Or, the union may retreat and regroup.

If the union is successful, you too have your options:

1. You may file an unfair labor practices charge against the
   union and attempt to have the election set aside. Of course,
   the charges must be substantial and supported by evidence.
2. You may sell your business and subject the purchaser to the
   burdens of a union shop, as well as any liability for pending
   charges of unfair labor practices.
3. You may go out of business, but closing down only part of it
   or moving out of state may be an illegal union avoidance
   scheme.
4. Or, most realistically, you may recognize the union and commence good-faith collective bargaining.

9.09   The Duty to Bargain

The Wagner Act requires an employer to "bargain collectively with
the representatives of his employees"; such bargaining is to be "in

respect to rates of pay, wages, hours of employment, or other conditions of employment." An amendment to the Taft-Hartley Act defines collective bargaining as follows:

> the performance of the mutual obligation of the employer and the representative of the employees to meet at reasonable times and confer in good faith with respect to wages, hours, and other terms and conditions of employment, or the negotiation of an agreement, or any question arising thereunder, and the execution of a written contract incorporating any agreement reached if requested by either party, but such obligation does not compel either party to agree to a proposal or require the making of a concession.

Bad faith, then, can be shown by "surface bargaining"—avoiding the real issues, delaying tactics, refusing to discuss "mandatory" issues (including wages, hours, fringes, union security, and plant rules), refusing to make counterproposals, or declaring an intent not to reach an agreement.

Any party found guilty of bad-faith bargaining by the NLRB can expect the assessment of penalties and economic retaliation in the form of a work stoppage. Employees may legally strike, but they may not conduct a wildcat strike or slowdown, nor may they strike in violation of an existing no-strike clause or an NLRB-declared sixty-day cooling-off period. Employees who strike because of their employer's bad-faith bargaining may have rights to reinstatement. An employer has the equivalent right to lockouts, a last-gasp weapon, which is technically regulated and, like a strike, brings economic suffering to both sides. For better or worse, a threatened or existing work stoppage may bring the Federal Mediation and Conciliation Service into the bargaining arena as a go-between.

9.10 The Union Contract

Whether negotiations come easily or not, the collective bargaining agreement should be your assurance of a smooth relationship with your employees throughout its term. Your attorney will negotiate from strength and fairness and will arrive at an agreement that both sides can live with. At least some of these issues will be resolved:

▶ *Conditions of recognition.* There will be a clear definition of which employees constitute the bargaining unit.

▶ *Union security.* Taft-Hartley requires that any so-called *check-off* provision authorizing union dues deductions from employer paychecks be included in the agreement and OKd by employees. A checkoff can cover only a one-year period. *Hot cargo clauses,* by which unions can refuse to handle struck work, are illegal altogether.

▶ *Union activities.* The ground rules for the conduct of union affairs will be fully set out.

▶ *Working conditions.* These may be the meat and potatoes of the agreement. Job classifications, subcontracting provisions, plant rules, hiring and firing, seniority systems—all these and more will be fully explored in the agreement.

▶ *Wages.* This topic may be covered in the contract proper or in an appendix or separate agreement that can more easily be reviewed annually and amended. Either way, the sticky issue of overtime and holidays and their respective rates of pay will be tackled.

▶ *Health and welfare benefits.* The agreement will include a detailed explanation of coverages and who is covered; Taft-Hartley will again control any payroll deductions. Company policy on sick leave, funeral leave, and jury duty will also be specified.

▶ *Management clause.* The rights and responsibilities of management will be itemized, as will the decision areas outside union jurisdiction.

▶ *Grievance procedure.* A grievance will be defined, along with the step-by-step procedure for its adjudication.

▶ *Arbitration procedure.* Again, the process will be exhaustively detailed and will include prearbitration procedures, time limits for arbitration requests, the scope of arbitrators' authority, the arbitrator selection method, and more.

▶ *No-strike and picket line clauses.* Careful drafting can eliminate the loopholes that often plague these areas.

▶ *Nondiscrimination clause.* The contract will comply with the equal employment opportunity laws (see sections 9.02 and 9.03).

9.11   The End Result

Again, there is a merger of objectives: Business meets its social obligations and, at the same time, provides its employees with opportunity, security, and status. Whether benefits and conditions are negotiated individually or collectively, the end result is a more fruitful employment relationship and, in the long run, a more successful business. So the law's requirements and the goals of the entrepreneur never need collide.

10 *Handling the Executive Team*

Say "we," "us" and "ours" when you're talking instead of "you fellows" and "I."

—Rudyard Kipling

10.01 Getting the Best

Management is leadership, and your ability to attract and develop top-notch people will have greater bearing on your success in business than anything else.

Your unique organization and operation of the management team can set you apart from your peers. Start at the beginning with a formal, contractual relationship with every team player who's got it in him to help make you a success. The substance of the contract will vary from business to business, but here are a few important topics, in addition to the pointers set out in Exhibit 9-1, that you and your lawyer should consider in drafting any executive employment agreement:

- ▶ *Duties and responsibilities.* Try to avoid duplication of effort, and agree right from the start about how much authority each executive is to have. But remember, the world turns, so reserve the right to make changes.
- ▶ *Best efforts.* Demand a full day's effort for full day's pay.
- ▶ *Noncompetition.* You should probably have a restrictive covenant such as the one shown in item 6, Exhibit 9-1, limiting competition or unfair competition for a reasonable time after employment ends. Federal or state law will strike down any clause held unreasonable in time or geography, so work with your lawyer in defining the minimum you need to be safe.

► *Trade secrets.* These are your property, and so are your customer lists. Have your key people acknowledge your ownership and grant you the right to injunctive relief for any infringement (see section 4.03).

► *Term.* Choose a short, fixed term to start; you can always renew. Also, retain the right to end the relationship for misconduct, nonperformance, disability, or other commonsense reasons such as the sale, merger, or discontinuance of your business.

► *Compensation.* Set out in great detail the base salary, any automatic adjustments, payment frequency, bonuses, deferred compensation, fringes, and forfeiture provisions. When stock is part of the package, the corporation should be given the "right of first refusal" of your employee's shares should he die, resign, retire, go bankrupt, or simply want to sell them. And he should be bound to join in the sale of stock in the event the corporation's controlling owners elect to sell out.

Cash on the Barrelhead

Attracting good employees involves obvious, but never simple, techniques. Design a compensation package that will give high-level employees the financial security and self-esteem they need to do a good job for you, and you will have no trouble recruiting and training all the talent you need. The executives who help you run your show will become highly motivated and will contribute to increased productivity and increased profits for all of you to share.

But developing a compensation package is rarely a simple task. Cash is the traditional way to pay employees, and regardless of changes in the federal tax laws, it is usually an easy and attractive way to compensate executives.

Bonuses and Deferred Compensation

After a realistic base salary, many businesses pay their executives *current cash bonuses* that are tied to company profits. The employee is thus given a genuine incentive, and the employer can deduct it all in the year it is paid. One disadvantage: Executives can claim current bonuses that aren't contingent upon future service and then move on to graze elsewhere.

One often proposed solution is the *deferred bonus,* paid over a period of years starting after it is earned, usually after retirement. A deferred bonus or other deferred compensation can be made expressly subject to forfeiture by an executive who engages in competition with your business or otherwise exposes it to loss. At first blush, deferral may appear especially desirable, since the employee may net more of his bonus dollars after retirement, when he might be in a lower tax bracket. But abandon that widely held belief. The likelihood is that a deferred bonus will be taxable at the same rate as a current bonus is, particularly if the retired executive will receive qualified retirement plan benefits and income from outside investments along with his deferred bonus.

The major limitation applicable to deferred compensation of all forms, including elections to defer income under any 401(k) plan (section 10.03), is that only up to $7,500, annually per employee under all these arrangements, can be deferred without losing the deduction/noninclusion tax benefits.

In weighing the relative merits of a deferred bonus plan, look at these problems too:

▶ The whole point of the plan—retaining your truly exceptional executives—can be undercut by a hungry competitor who is willing to match your deferred payout.

▶ Your top executives may resent your padlocking them.

▶ They may question your ability to pay up when their time comes.

▶ Employees will gripe about your eventual payment in discounted inflated dollars. One answer: In the interim, invest the deferred funds for them.

▶ A forfeiture clause can backfire, forcing a marginal employee to stay when he might otherwise leave.

Sharing Your Shares

Another way to foster longevity among corporate executives is through the use of *stock options.* Grant your key employees the right to buy shares of your company's stock at a bargain price. The catch is that if they engage in competition with your business or otherwise expose it to loss, the right to exercise the options is forfeited. If the options meet certain qualification requirements, it is only after the options are exercised and the risk of forfeiture lapses that your employees must pay a tax on the difference between the value of their shares then and the amount they paid for them. If the options are not qualified under such requirements, another benefit is available: As the employees recognize gain when exercising their options, the company can deduct equal amounts as compensation expense.

Stock options provide a means of compensation that does not require an employer to spend its cash assets. Employees, on the other hand, appreciate the opportunity to participate in the growth of the company that is available through stock options. At the shareholder level, however, the real economic effect of granting stock options is not significantly different from that of paying cash bonuses, since both transactions dilute stock values to about the same extent. On the other hand, shareholder preferences are usually given as the reason for choosing stock options rather than cash bonuses in arranging incentive compensation for executives.

One explanation for the shareholder preference for stock options, particularly for small businesses, is the avoidance of external financing that the options facilitate, in contrast to the payment of bonuses that may require bank or other loans. In any event, it is estimated that more than nine out of ten corporations having more than one shareholder do use some form of stock options.

The two basic forms of stock options are *incentive stock options* (*ISOs* or qualified options) and *nonqualified* options. While ISOs had, before the Tax Reform Act of 1986, superior tax treatment advantages as against nonqualified options, two different provisions of that Act combined in such a way as to effectively reverse the relative tax advantages of the two forms of options.

One of these reversal-causing provisions is the individual alternative minimum tax (AMT), under which the exercising of an ISO gives rise to a *preference*, or an amount subject to the minimum tax. The other provision is the removal of the previously lower tax rate for long-term capital gains, in comparison to ordinary income. An example illustrating the differences in tax treatment of the two kinds of options before and after the 1986 Act, is set out in Exhibit 10-1.

Exhibit 10-1. Illustration of taxation of stock options before and after the Tax Reform Act of 1986.

Assume a corporate executive has a salary of $100,000 and is granted 10,000 options at $20 per share. The options do not have a readily ascertainable fair market value in the year that the options are granted. After a mandatory time elapses, the value of the stock rises to $40 a share, and the options are exercised. A year later, the executive sells out for $50 a share and realizes a $300,000 gain. The following chart compares the tax treatment for this executive before and after the 1986 Act:

	Tax	
	Old Law	*New Law*
ISOs	$ 62,000	$118,475
Nonqualified options	200,000	84,000

The computation shown, in the case of the ISOs, reflects the $200,000 preference triggered under the AMT in the year of exercising the options. The AMT for that year, in the absence of other preferences, is $34,475, an amount based on rates becoming effective in 1989 under the 1986 Act. The balance of the tax is the 28% rate, under the 1986 Act, on the $300,000 gain realized in the year of sale. As to the nonqualified options, the executive owes 28% of the $200,000 "paper" gain in the year of exercise, and 28% of the gain not previously taxed, or $100,000, in the year of sale.

The amount of ISOs that can be exercised in one year cannot exceed $100,000. The other conditions relating to ISOs are as follows:

1. The employee must, to avoid tax in the year he exercises his option, hold the stock for a minimum of two years after the option is granted and for one year after the option is exercised.
2. The employee must have received the option for some reason connected with his employment and must remain employed by the company issuing the option from the time of issuance until three months before the option is exercised.

3. The term of the option may not exceed ten years.
4. The option price must be no less than the fair market value of the stock on the date of issuance (a good-faith attempt to value the stock accurately must be made).
5. The option must be transferable by inheritance only.
6. The option plan must specify the aggregate number of shares that may be issued and the employees eligible to receive the option.
7. The option must be granted within ten years of the earlier of the date of adoption of the plan or the date it was approved by the shareholders.
8. If the employee owns more than 10 percent of the company, the option price must be at least 110 percent of the market value, and its term may not exceed five years.

The tax advantages of an ISO before the Tax Reform Act of 1986 were twofold: (1) that no gain was taxable until the employee-holder had both exercised the option and sold—possibly years after the exercise—the stock so obtained and (2) the imposition of tax at long-term capital gains rates, which were previously lower than the regular tax rates. The two advantages for ISOs were offset somewhat by the rule that the employer was not entitled to any expense deductions in granting the options.

The value of a nonqualified option, both before and after the 1986 Act, is taxed as ordinary income to the employee for the year when it is granted if it then has an ascertainable fair market value. If, as is often the case with small businesses, a nonqualified option has no readily ascertainable fair market value at the time it is granted, it won't be subject to regular income taxes until it is exercised by the employee, with gain being realized equal to the appreciation in the value of the underlying stock since the year that the option was granted. However, part of the tax story in the case of nonqualified options is the tax on the difference between the option price, which then becomes the basis of the stock acquired in such exercise, and the net proceeds in the year the acquired shares are sold. This last-mentioned component of taxed gain to the employee is deferred until the year the shares are sold. However, the amount of gain so recognized is not a deductible expense for the employer. Except for this nondeductible amount, and for another exception relating to *unreasonable compensation* (section 10.02), tax law provides generally that when the employee recognizes income for tax purposes in receiving or exercising a nonqualified option, the employer is entitled to a deduction for the same amount as ordinary and necessary business expense. If part of the amount of nonqualified options granted by an employer is determined by the IRS to be unreasonable compensation, the employer will not be entitled to any business expense deduction for such excess.

Other Option Variations

Resist coming to the conclusion that all your compensation choices are hopelessly muddled and ineffective. Clearly, conflicting tax and business objectives will force you into some fancy footwork, and no option approach will be ideal. Creative lawyers are forever devising new ways of meeting those often inconsistent challenges. Here are two option variations, other than ISOs and nonqualified options, that may be worth investigating:

1. *Phantom stock plans and stock appreciation rights plans.* These plans grant to select employees hypothetical shares of stock plus, in the case of phantom stock plans, the dividends they would earn. At a later date, the dollar amount of appreciation in the market value of the shares (and their phantom earnings in phantom stock plans) over their value when they were credited to employee accounts is paid out in cash. This is a deferred cash bonus, with appreciation in corporate stock measuring most or all of the amount of the payout. Phantom stock plans and stock appreciation rights plans are favored by publicly held companies, which need not determine a "market value" by formula; closely held companies usually opt for a deferred cash plan.

2. *Employee stock ownership or bonus plan.* Options issued under a stock bonus plan or employee stock ownership plan (ESOP) may qualify for special tax treatment, but discrimination in favor of top-level employees is not permitted. An employer can take deductions when making contributions to a qualified stock bonus plan,

but if the plan is not qualified, deductions are available only when the cash or property (the stock) is actually made available to employees; otherwise, the employee's rights become transferable or not subject to a substantial risk of forfeiture.

Perks: Important Choices

No longer do "dollars now" and "dollars then" constitute the enlightened employer's compensation program. Yesterday's fringes are today's indispensables. Yet every business is plagued by the competing demands of cash outflow, capital requirements, and earnings objectives, and every business must relate its net after-tax cost of employee salaries and perquisites to employees' net after-tax benefits. While not long ago self-employed proprietors could not take any deduction for the cost of health insurance to cover themselves, their spouses, and dependents, the law now recognizes, at least in part, the business implications of health insurance and allows up to 25 percent of the premiums to be deducted. For corporate employers, there are health plans and other perks—tax-free to the employee (assuming the tax rules are complied with) but deductible by the employer—that are particularly cost effective:

▶ *Medical/disability/dental plans.* Whether a self-insured or externally insured plan is chosen, the ability to use pretax dollars to cover medical expenses remains a key, if not the major, reason to incorporate a small business. A basic group health insurance plan is an indispensable fringe for employees, their spouses, and dependent children and for ex-employees (until they are covered by other health insurance), their spouses, and dependent children. Pursuant to a written plan, a corporation may also pay or reimburse any health costs of eligible corporate employees and deduct its full out-of-pocket expense on a self-insured basis. Most health plans, other than certain plans provided by statute, can meet nondiscrimination rules in one of two ways, either (1) satisfying an 80 percent coverage test or (2) meeting a three-prong eligibility test plus a benefits test. As to ex-employees who elect to continue coverage after discharge or retirement, the employer may charge a premium of up to 102 percent of the amount of the cost to the plan for comparable individuals who are still employed (and who may or may not be required to contribute to plan costs).

▶ *Executive bonus insurance.* As a fringe benefit that can discriminate in favor of key people, an executive bonus insurance plan can provide personal life coverage at nominal cost to the employees, and, if the expense is an ordinary and necessary amount, the employer can deduct its payment of the premiums. The nominal cost to the employees arises because the amounts of the premiums are includable in their taxable incomes unless the sole benefit is a death benefit of $5,000 or less. After paying the premiums, the corporation has no rights in or control over the policy. Flexibility is gained not only through the ability to select which employees will be eligible but also by (1) arranging a premium schedule that dovetails with available cash flow in the corporation and (2) enabling the executive to choose among whole, endowment, or universal life, with variable or fixed premiums and annuity or lump-sum payouts. These plans are often desirable or necessary as a means to fund a cross-purchase or buy-sell agreement (see section 2.04).

▶ *Group life.* A corporation can deduct the premiums for up to $50,000 in group term insurance on the lives of at least ten employees or retired employees, and those employees will realize no taxable income unless taxable payouts are received from the insurance company. Beyond $50,000, the corporation may still take a tax deduction, but the employee or retired employee pays a tax on the value of the premiums for the coverage in excess of the $50,000—still a tax-favored bargain. The nondiscrimination requirements applicable to health plans also apply to the group life plans.

▶ *Split-dollar life.* Split-dollar insurance can be purchased by an employer who pays only part of the premium, usually a part that represents the increase in cash value; the employee pays the balance. The policy taken out is whole life insurance, with the proceeds being payable to the corporation (to the extent of its investment) and to the employee's beneficiary. There are, when setting up a split-dollar plan, many different ways in which premium expense can be split and proceeds paid out, depending on the particular circumstances. Although the antidiscrimination rules governing most types of plans do not apply, a split-dollar plan is subject to the Employment Retirement Income Security Act (ERISA), and therefore must meet specified plan requirements, reporting and disclosure rules, and fiduciary standards.

▶ *Permanent injury/disability retirement benefits.* Certain low-income elderly and totally disabled persons are eligible for tax credits of up to 15 percent of payments they receive under disability retirement plans. Within prescribed limitations, the costs of providing such plans are deductible expenses for employers, and employees are only taxed upon their receipt of benefits.

▶ *Cafeteria plans.* Employer contributions under a written plan (generally referred to as a *cafeteria plan*) that permits employees to elect between taxable and nontaxable benefits, or between cash compensation and such benefits, are excluded from the taxable incomes of the employees to the extent that nontaxable benefits are elected. The availability of such choices on a nondiscriminatory basis does not trigger the application of the *constructive receipt* rule as to compensation that could be received but is waived in favor of nontaxable benefits. The constructive receipt rule generally applies whenever taxable compensation is receivable, but the prospective recipient asks the obligor to delay making payment.

▶ *Fringe benefits generally.* An employee can exclude from income fringe benefits that qualify in four categories:
1. No-additional-cost services, such as free trips for airline employees
2. Qualified employee discounts, up to 20 percent, from the price of goods or services provided by the employer
3. Working condition fringes, such as parking privileges on or near the place of business, use of subsidized eating facilities, or the use by an employee of a company car or airplane for business purposes
4. "De minimis" (miniscule) fringes, such as incidental personal use (under 15 percent of the total) of a company

        photocopying machine, occasional supper money or taxi
        fare because of overtime work, holiday gifts with a low fair
        market value, or free coffee and doughnuts

While antidiscrimination rules apply to many of these fringes, such
as subsidized eating facilities, many of the working condition fringes
may discriminate—a salesperson may have a need to use a company
car that a staff worker would not.

▶ *Dependent care assistance program.* An employer can deduct
as business expense amounts paid or incurred under a *dependent
care assistance program*, which is a plan to assist a single parent or
families with certain dependents and having a need of employment
for both spouses (in married households). Employees may exclude
from their taxable incomes up to $5,000 each year in dependent
care benefits, whether received as employer-provided services at an
employer location or at an independent day care center, or as reimbursement of the employee's expenses. In general, the dependents
must be under age 15, except that expenses for a parent needing
out-of-home care but spending at least eight hours in the employee's home can also be reimbursed. An independent day care center
must provide day care for more than six individuals. Up to $960 in
annual tax credits for dependent care may be available to employees
in the absence of an employer program, and the employees of some
small businesses, depending on family earnings situations, could
come out ahead if the employer does not have a dependent care
program.

▶ *Moving expenses.* The expenses incurred in house hunting, in
renting temporary lodging, and in selling an old residence and purchasing a new one are generally deductible by the employer and the
employee as a working condition fringe benefit. The employer may
not deduct from its income, and the employee cannot exclude from
his income, certain nonqualified moving expenses such as paying
brokerage commissions, reimbursing a loss that the employee incurs
in selling his former residence, extra compensation to offset a
higher interest rate under a new mortgage, or redecorating expenses
that the employer pays.

▶ *Education.* The cost of in-house seminars is tax deductible by the employer and tax free to the employee, and this treatment also extends to nondiscriminatory tuition reduction programs of educational institutions for their own employees. Grants for outside study are deductible too, but only if the expenditures are job related and improve employee skills without qualifying them for new occupations or if the expenditures meet certain rules covering scholarships and fellowships.

▶ *Travel and entertainment.* Reasonable expenses in promoting the employer's business are deductible by it and are tax free to the employee, except that 20 percent of the cost of business meals and entertainment is not deductible and the other 80 percent is deductible only if the employer or a representative is present when the expense is incurred. Luxury water travel, travel as education, and travel for charitable purposes are subject to special rules. The costs of attending a convention are deductible if incurred in the active conduct of a trade or business, but not as an expense related to the production of investment income. There are strict rules as to documenting the time, place, purpose, and participants for all such expenses.

▶ *Meals and lodging for convenience of employer.* In general, an employee may exclude from gross income the value of meals and lodging if furnished by an employer on its premises for its convenience. To qualify for such exclusion, it must be a condition of employment that the meals or lodging, or both, take place on the business premises.

▶ *Automobiles and airplanes.* An employer can depreciate a company car or airplane and deduct all its running costs. The employee receives taxable income only to the extent the unit is put to more-than-incidental personal use, except that in the case of an airplane, there is no recognized exclusion for any incidental personal use (which also reduces the amount of the depreciation and expense deductions for the corporation). One further note: When a passenger or driver of a company car is a shareholder-employee, the corporation may not deduct the personal use portion of the car depreciation and expenses.

▶ *Financial advice.* The employer may deduct the cost of employee counseling if the expense can be supported as reasonable and necessary to the business, but the employee realizes reportable taxable income equal to its value on his personal tax return. Financial counseling may increase spendable employee income and thus sweeten the whole compensation package.

▶ *Legal services.* Employees can, under an employee plan, receive legal services, either prepaid or postpaid depending on the plan terms. The costs to the employer of making the plan available are deductible to it if the expense can be supported as reasonable and necessary, but the employees are deemed to receive additional personal income.

▶ *Other job-related benefits.* Other job-related fringes may include expense accounts and memberships in social clubs or business or professional associations. To the extent that the expenditures are solely made, used for reasonable and necessary business purposes, and subject to limitations on discriminating among classes of employees, the employer can deduct them, and the employee need not include them in personal income.

▶ *Other personal benefits.* Depending on the need to attract and keep employees, a company may deduct the expense of low- or no-interest loans, free medical checkups, paid vacations, pregnancy or other leaves with or without any stipends, personal holidays, and other miscellaneous benefits. Some, but not all, of these benefits are excludable from employee income as working condition or de minimis fringes.

10.02 When *You* Are the Employee

A nondeductible expense costs substantially more than a deductible one, so tax deductibility can maximize the output of every dollar you budget for the upper echelon—including yourself. The Internal Revenue Code allows an employer to deduct "expenses paid or incurred during the taxable year in carrying on any trade or business, including a reasonable allowance for personal services actually rendered."

What is "reasonable" and when compensation is "for personal services actually rendered" are issues the IRS frequently raises in claiming that a corporate shareholder-employee's paycheck is really a disguised nondeductible dividend. Special tax rules on *golden parachutes* illustrate the general problem in this area, namely, what is "excess" beyond a "reasonable" amount?

A golden parachute indicates an arrangement that provides *excessive* severance payments to one or more executives at the time of a change in ownership or control of the corporation. A 20 percent excise tax applies to the recipient of excess parachute payments, and the corporate employer cannot deduct the excess amounts. Payments are "excessive" to the extent that they exceed three times a *base amount*. The base amount is the average of compensation paid to the individual in question during the five taxable years before the change in ownership or control.

In the interest of safeguarding the tax deductibility of the compensation paid to your executives, you should take these steps:

1. At least annually, adopt a compensation package by a resolution of the directors (one of whom might well be independent). Define its elements, and cite its underlying philosophy.
2. Record any special factors justifying big salaries: long hours of work, unique abilities, experience and qualifications, and any other employee pluses. The IRS will consider these, along with industry comparisons and economic conditions, in judging "reasonableness."
3. Establish a clear dividend policy; that way, salaries will less likely be viewed as hiding a return on your business investment. Many small corporations pay a token dividend every year just to help counter such a challenge.
4. The directors should authorize any bonuses, and employment contracts should support any contingent payments to employees, especially shareholder-employees.
5. Finally, the corporation should enter into *reimbursement*

agreements with all shareholder-employees such as the following:

> Compensation payments or reimbursements made to the officer that are disallowed, in whole or in part, as a deductible expense by the Internal Revenue Service shall be reimbursed by him to the full extent of the disallowance. It shall be the duty of the Board of Directors to enforce the repayment of each such amount disallowed. A payment shall be deemed to be disallowed only when the time has lapsed for an appeal from or review of the adverse decision of the last tribunal or agency to consider the issue.

If compensation is deemed nondeductible by the corporation, it is returned and made available for redistribution at another time, and perhaps in another way.

10.03   Company Retirement Plans

The bedrock of any compensation package is usually the company retirement program. The prominence of retirement planning as a high-level compensation tool derives from the "qualification" of certain formalized retirement programs. Qualified retirement plans are those that meet rigid IRS standards and the sweeping tax and labor principles of ERISA. Corporate employer contributions to a qualified plan are currently deductible; the earnings of such contributions grow tax free; benefiting employees defer personal taxation on their allocable shares of both contributions and earnings until later in life; and funds are made available at a time when their need may be greatest.

A Dozen Demands

Here are the basic requirements for a qualified retirement program:

1. The plan must be formally established by the employer on a permanent basis. If a plan is terminated within a few years after it is started, then the plan may be deemed not to have been estab-

lished on a permanent basis—and treated as if it had never been qualified even if all the other requirements were met.

2. The plan must be communicated to the employees.

3. It must be maintained for the exclusive benefit of employees and their beneficiaries.

4. The plan must be nondiscriminatory in coverage, and, in particular, may not discriminate in favor of certain individuals such as officers or a person owning 5 percent or more of the corporation's stock. Generally, (1) 70 percent of all employees must be covered or (2) 70 percent of all employees must be eligible and 80 percent of all eligible employees covered.

5. The plan must be nondiscriminatory in operation, too, so contributions, benefits, and forfeitures cannot be allocated or distributed in a way that favors shareholder-employees and managers.

6. Ordinarily, employees must become eligible to participate after one year of service or upon reaching age 21, whichever comes later.

7. All employee contributions, and the benefits accruing thereon, must "vest" (become absolutely theirs) immediately, and the benefits accruing from employer contributions must vest 100 percent upon a participant's completion of five years of service or in accordance with this schedule:

Years of Service	Percentage Vested
3	20%
4	40
5	60
6	80
7	100

Even more rapid vesting is required if a plan is *top-heavy.* "Top-heavy" basically refers to a plan in which certain key employees have accumulated 60 percent or more of the contributions or benefits under the plan.

8. The plan must provide for two types of annuity payouts of benefits, a *qualified joint and survivor annuity* (QJSA) and a *qualified preretirement survivor annuity* (QPSA). A QJSA basically applies to married participants who die after retiring, whereas a QPSA applies to married participants who die prior to retirement. Under the QJSA, the retired participant receives payments for a designated period or for life, and upon his death, the beneficiary receives payments for the rest of the period or life. Under the QPSA, there is no initial payout of benefits prior to death, but otherwise the payout method generally follows the QJSA. Either type of payout can be waived by participants, with the consent of their spouses if they are married, in accordance with narrowly defined procedures and notices.

9. The plan must not exceed statutory limits on contributions and benefits. In *defined-contribution plans* (profit-sharing and stock bonus plans) and money purchase pension plans, annual contributions for a participant under *all* qualified plans cannot exceed the lesser of $30,000 or 25 percent of the year's total compensation, with certain additions for cost-of-living changes after 1986, and with only compensation up to $200,000 being considered.

In *defined-benefit pension plans*, annual benefits, funded in accordance with statute, may not exceed $90,000 or 100 percent of compensation, whichever is lower, with additions for cost-of-living changes after 1986 and adjustments for retirements before or after age 65.

10. Plan assets other than insurance contracts must be held in a trust managed by a bank, insurance company, or bonded fiduciary. The trustee is obliged to act for the exclusive benefit of plan participants as a "prudent man" would, conservatively diversifying his portfolio. And, among other things, it is the trustee's duty to avoid suspect trust transactions with himself, with the employer and its officers, with directors, and with 10 percent shareholders. These transactions might include any sale, exchange, or lease of property; the lending of money or any extension of credit; and the furnishing of goods, most services, and facilities.

11. Qualification carries with it all kinds of reporting obligations. After IRS approval, participants must receive a clear summary of the plan, including vesting standards. An annual report must also be filed with the IRS, and actuarial reports for defined-benefit plans must be filed at least every three years. The Pension Benefit Guarantee Corporation, the insurer of vested benefits for all defined-benefit plans except professional service corporation plans, also requires annual reports, as well as notice of any impending curtailment or termination of benefits.

12. Should the plan be terminated, participants must be fully vested in their accrued benefits, and assets must be allocated according to ERISA guidelines.

Variations on the Theme

The requirements for a retirement program are sticky, and the variations are many. Let's look at a few of the most popular concepts and see what they have to offer you:

▶ *Profit-sharing plans.* Your corporation can contribute and deduct a slice of its profits—up to 15 percent of its payroll—to a trust. Decide exactly how much to contribute each year; you need not commit yourself to a specific formula as long as contributions are substantial and recurring. The trustee will credit each participant's individual account with his share of any employer contribution and its tax-exempt earnings; the participant may supplement the corporate contribution with a voluntary employee contribution, which also earns him tax-free investment income. Upon an employee's death, retirement, or disability, all that's in his account will be used to purchase an annuity or otherwise distributed, depending on the election and beneficiary designation of the employee and any required spousal consent.

▶ *Money-purchase pensions.* You may make mandatory contributions equal to a percentage of the eligible participants' compensation and deduct them; the percentage cannot, when added to the percentage rate of contributions under other qualified plans, exceed 25 percent. Although the contributions are required even if there are not profits in a given year, this type of plan closely resembles the profit-sharing plan format. Each participant's pension will be whatever could be purchased as an annuity by the amount in his individual account, including earnings, on hand at his retirement.

▶ *Stock bonus plans and ESOPs.* In qualified stock bonus plans and ESOPs, employees truly share in the ownership of corporate capital. Under a stock bonus plan, discretionary employer contributions are made in cash form that is used to purchase employer stock, whereas an ESOP usually shortens that procedure so that employer stock is directly contributed. In most other respects the two types of plans are the same. Distributions must be made in employer stock; otherwise, these plans work like profit-sharing plans or combined profit-sharing/money-purchase plans. An ESOP can be either a *tax credit ESOP* or a *leveraged ESOP.* A tax credit ESOP may be any type of defined contribution plan, other than a money-purchase pension plan alone. A leveraged ESOP may be only a stock bonus plan or a combination stock bonus and money purchase plan. Participants must be allowed to elect partial diversification of their accounts so that they do not hold employer securities exclusively, and independent appraisers must make all valuations of nonreadily tradable employer securities. Although these plans may entail dilution of your shareholdings, they also qualify for special exceptions to general plan prohibitions on making loans to the corporate employer, with the result that your corporation can borrow money repayable in pretax dollars and, at the same time, increase cash flow, refinance debts, and supply a ready market for corporate stock (see section 12.03)

▶ *401(k) plans.* A profit-sharing or stock bonus plan may include a *401(k),* or *cash or deferred plan.* Such a plan is one in which a participant may elect between having compensation paid in cash directly to the employee or having an equivalent amount put into a profit-sharing or stock bonus plan. Often, an employer agrees to make partially matching plan contributions based on the amount of the employee's plan contributions. Also, employees might be allowed to make contributions beyond the amounts that the employer can allocate on a tax-free basis. There is a $7,000 annual limit on the tax-free allocations—this being cumulative with all other forms of deferred compensation—and antidiscrimination and other restrictions apply. However, with the tightening of restrictions on individual retirement accounts (IRAs) (section 10.04 on "IRAs"), 401(k) plans are widely used and highly regarded by many employers and employees.

▶ *Pensions.* Your plan must be based on actuarially computed deductible contributions and provide benefits based on compensation, years of service, or both. Actuarial gains will reduce future corporate pay-ins. And tax-favored distributions will be paid out to retirees, the disabled, and beneficiaries of employees who die while in your company's service.

10.04   Retirement Planning for the Self-Employed

So much for the corporation. What about the proprietor and the partner? They too are eligible for a tax-sheltered retirement program. Although these programs are often referred to as HR-10 or Keogh plans, their only significant difference from the corporate plans is that there is no stock, and therefore no stock bonus plan or ESOP for proprietors and partners.

Meet IRA
Is everyone covered? Unfortunately not. Congress was well aware that millions of Americans did not participate in qualified retirement plans when, as part of ERISA, it allowed them to set up their own *individual retirement accounts* (IRAs). IRAs have filled a big security void (1) for people whose employers offer no qualified plan, (2) through a special IRA rollover feature, for employees whose employers have terminated their plans, and (3) ironically, for proprietors and partners who prefer to salt away retirement dollars without subsidizing the benefit for every three-year veteran in their shops. However, the ability to exclude contributions to IRAs

from taxable income is generally permitted only to individuals with adjusted gross income (before considering IRA contributions) below $25,000 for unmarried individuals and $40,000 for married individuals filing a joint return and, on less advantageous terms, to individuals with up to $10,000 more income than those amounts.

Basically, IRAs work this way:

▶ Each year, an eligible person may contribute up to $2,000 ($4,000 for married couples) to a trust or custodial account or, for annuity contracts, U.S. Retirement Bonds or gold or silver coins issued by the United States. Alternately, you may contribute up to $2,250 to an IRA that has a subaccount for the benefit of your spouse who does little or no work outside the home. If neither you nor your spouse participates in any other qualified plan, or if your income(s) are below the amounts described above, you may deduct these contributions from your income, or you may decide to make nondeductible contributions so that earnings can accumulate on a tax-free basis until your retirement or death.

▶ You may deduct your contributions, to the extent they're deductible, from your gross income "above the line" and not as an itemized deduction.

▶ Contributions grow tax free until distribution.

▶ Your account balance will be distributed to you beginning at an age between 59½ and 70½ (or upon death or disability)—penalties apply to both early and late withdrawals. A uniform recovery of basis rule applies, so that part of each distribution is treated partially as a return of deductible contribution, of nondeductible contribution, and of earnings, depending on the account history.

10.05 A Closing Comment

The mainstays of a solid organization are fairness and humanity. Take, but give too. Inspire your team to put out all that it can. Offer a reasonable, cost-effective, and motivating income package, and respond to the economic hazards of death, retirement, illness, and disability. Not only will you enhance your top employees' satisfaction with their work, but you will meet your social responsibilities in a way the outside world will commend. The employer, the employee, and the community will all become the beneficiaries of a profitable business strategy.

11 Protecting Corporate Officers and Directors From Liability

The successful executive is the man who can make money and stay out of the bankruptcy court.

—Knute Rockne

11.01 Risky Business

As a result of certain legal developments, you and the key executives of your corporation may encounter substantial personal liabilities in the course of performing responsibilities as directors and officers. You may find yourself named as defendant in a lawsuit that alleges the breach of statutory or common-law duties.

To secure the services of key people, you may have to agree to protect them from personal legal exposures. Fortunately, there are a number of steps you can take:

1. Be sure you and your executives understand legal requirements relating to dividends, accumulations of earnings, and the duties of care and loyalty (see sections 11.02, 11.03, and 11.04).

2. Advise your officers and directors that they must not profit personally from corporate business through matters that involve a conflict between their personal interest and that of the corporation, or appropriate for themselves personally opportunities that belong to the corporation (see section 11.05).

3. Be sure that your officers and directors know what their responsibilities are with regard to federal securities laws concerning inside information, adequate disclosure, sale of securities, due diligence, and buying or selling control in the corporation (see section 11.06).

4. Determine if the state in which your corporation is incorporated has available statutory provisions limiting officer or director liability (see section 11.07).

5. Review existing insurance coverage of all corporate officers and directors (see section 11.08).

6. Consider indemnifying corporate officers and directors in the bylaws (see section 11.09).

7. Study the checklist of laws imposing personal liabilities on corporate executives, set out in Exhibit 11-1.

11.02   Dividends

You and the directors of your corporation are prohibited by law from improper dividends. All fifty states have enacted statutes that impose personal liability, sometimes adding fines and imprisonment in criminal cases, upon directors who vote for or approve the declaration of improper dividends. Many of these laws also provide for shareholder liability in certain circumstances.

A dividend is improperly made if corporate assets are transferred to one or more shareholders in a distribution that is:

Exhibit 11-1. Checklist of laws imposing personal liability on corporate executives.

☐ Laws dealing with tax withholding, minimum wages, and overtime
☐ Equal employment regulations*
☐ Occupational safety laws*
☐ Environmental protection laws
☐ Credit regulations**
☐ Laws regarding pension and other benefit plans***
☐ Regulations regarding loans to company employees
☐ Special requirements or duties for regulated industries, such as food and drug businesses

*See Chapter 9.
**See Chapter 6.
***See Chapter 10.

▶ Made from funds not legally available for the purpose;
▶ Authorized without formal board approval;
▶ Disproportionately paid to fewer than all shareholders without proper authorization; or
▶ Made with fraudulent intent.

Usually, the requirements encompass any improper distributions or transfers and extend to a corporation's purchase of its own shares, improper distribution of assets during liquidation, and other acts such as making loans secured by shares of the corporation or commencing business operations before having the required capital.

A director's liability for an improper dividend is *joint and several*, meaning that the complaining party—either the corporation or a shareholder on its behalf—may sue you, another director, or any combination of directors responsible for the alleged improper dividend. Shareholders may act on behalf of the corporation derivatively, or a receiver, trustee in bankruptcy, or liquidator may sue in the right of the corporation. If you or another director is required by a court to pay more than a pro rata share of the judgment, you or such director may seek contribution from the other liable directors.

Various corporation statute provisions may protect you and the other directors from liability. You may defend yourself on the basis that you relied upon company documents before declaring the dividend, that you did not approve the action, or that the governing statute of limitations had expired.

You and the other directors are allowed to declare dividends or make other distributions in reliance on accounting and other records and reports compiled in the ordinary course of the corporation's business. This reliance must, however, be in good faith without knowledge or notice of facts indicating that reliance would be unwarranted. If you have no reason to suspect that company books and records are other than accurate reflections of the corporation's financial status, you may properly conclude from them that funds are available from which a dividend may be paid. As a director, you have a duty of care (section 11.04) that also requires you to read and analyze the supporting documents before voting to approve a dividend.

Only those directors voting for or assenting to a dividend will incur liability for improperly declaring it. If you were present at a board meeting at which dividends were declared and voted against the declaration, you cannot be found liable for declaring the dividend. However, a director present at such a meeting who abstains from voting on the dividend issue is nevertheless presumed to have assented to the declaration unless his dissent is recorded in the minutes prior to the meeting's adjournment or is forwarded to the secretary of the corporation soon after the board meeting.

A dividend paid to a shareholder may be recovered in various ways as follows:

▶ In a derivative suit filed by other shareholders on behalf of the corporation on the ground that the recipients of the dividend had knowledge that it was not properly authorized to be paid disproportionately to fewer than all shareholders.

▶ By a corporation's receiver, liquidator, trustee in bankruptcy, or creditors' committee or representatives, on the ground that the dividend payment was made during the corporation's insolvency or in a manner that rendered the corporation insolvent. The basis for this type of recovery may be provided in your state's corporation law or in your state's law of fraudulent conveyances.

▶ By the creditors of an insolvent corporation on the basis of a common-law right to recover amounts paid to shareholders that were needed instead to pay corporate obligations. Although this type of case is rare during the normal course of business, creditors have often recovered against shareholders who have received liquidating dividends or have otherwise withdrawn assets from a corporation in such a way as to render corporate debts uncollectable.

11.03 Accumulation of Earnings

A penalty tax is imposed on your corporation's accumulated taxable income if your corporation was formed or availed of for the purpose of avoiding income taxes at the shareholder level. The tax is not a personal obligation of corporate shareholders, directors, or officers in the first instance, but the enforcement of the tax can lead to legal actions against you if you have received amounts that should have been used to pay the tax obligations. Thus, you should have a basic understanding of the *accumulated earnings tax*, which is the usual name for this penalty, just for your personal protection.

As a statutory exemption, your corporation can accumulate up to $250,000 ($150,000 for a personal service corporation) of undistributed earnings and profits without being subject to the tax. The tax on any excess accumulation has two tiers. First, there is a tax at a rate of 27½ percent on *accumulated taxable income* not in excess of $100,000. Then, at the second level, there is a tax of 38½ percent of *accumulated taxable income* that exceeds $100,000. "Accumulated taxable income" is the taxable income to the corporation after certain adjustments, reductions, and credits specified in the Internal Revenue Code.

The tax presupposes a deliberate purpose on the part of the corporation to evade shareholder taxes. The primary issues are whether your retaining surplus earnings is reasonable and what business reasons you have for not distributing net income to shareholders in the form of dividends. If no business purpose is evident for an accumulation, or definite plans have not been made for its use, the surtax can be assessed. However, if your corporation has retained large profits based on your business judgment that it has a need for large working capital or other major outlays, you may have a valid defense against the tax.

For working capital requirements, a rule of thumb called the *Bardahl formula* (arising from an actual case involving Bardahl Manufacturing Corp.) has been successfully established on the basis of an operating cycle worksheet set forth in Exhibit 11-2.

You may be able to successfully show that accumulations of earnings are necessary for one of the following purposes, any of which may be an acceptable alternative to working capital requirements:

▸ Meeting competition
▸ Planning for business reverses
▸ Meeting contingent liabilities
▸ Furnishing funds for expansion

Exhibit 11-2. Operating cycle worksheet.

Step 1: Determine the operating
cycle percentage.

A. Inventory turnover percentage:
   (i) Inventory beginning of
       year   S_____
   (ii) Inventory end of year   _____
   (iii) Average inventory,
        (i) + (ii)/2   S_____
   (iv) Cost of goods sold   _____
   (v) Inventory turnover per-
       centage, (iii)/(iv)   _____%

B. Accounts receivable turnover percentage:
   (i) Accounts receivable be-
       ginning of year   S_____
   (ii) Accounts receivable end
        of year   _____
   (iii) Average accounts receiv-
        able, (i) + (ii)/2   S_____
   (iv) Total sales   _____
   (v) Accounts receivable per-
       centage, (iii)/(iv)   _____%

C. Operating cycle percentage =
   A(v) + B(v)   _____%

Step 2: Determine necessary working capital.

D. Operating expenses for year:
   (i) Cost of goods sold   S_____
   (ii) Other operating expenses   _____
   (iii) Federal income taxes   _____
   (iv) Add (i) through (iv)   _____
   (v) Less depreciation   —   (_____)
   (vi) Total operating expenses
        (iv) − (v)   S_____

Necessary working capital, C × D(vi) =   S_____

On the other hand, certain circumstances may indicate that your purpose is to avoid income tax on earnings distributed to shareholders. The IRS will give close scrutiny to factors such as:

- ► The extent to which your corporation has distributed its profits
- ► Dealings between your corporation and your shareholders (such as personal loans to directors or other shareholders, or the expenditure of corporate funds for the personal benefit of shareholders)
- ► The investment by your corporation of undistributed earnings in assets having no reasonable connection with your business

11.04   Duties of Care and Loyalty

Your officers and directors have a legal obligation to serve the corporation in accordance with legally imposed duties of care and loyalty. In general, these duties require your executives to act in good faith and with the care an ordinarily prudent person would exercise under similar circumstances. The characteristics that the law expects in an individual being considered for election as a director include:

- ► Independence
- ► An inquisitive nature
- ► Honesty and helpfulness
- ► Broad business experience
- ► Cooperativeness balanced with assertiveness

If a lawsuit is brought, the performance of your directors will be measured by standards such as these:

- ► Regular attendance at board and committee meetings
- ► Review of (and questions regarding, when necessary) corporate minutes, financial statements, and other material given them at or between meetings
- ► Participation in discussions held during board meetings

(whether such discussions were of major or minor import, but with greater emphasis on significant plans and proposals)

► Independent inquiry when necessary and the obtaining of information sufficient to permit informed decisions
► Registration of appropriate objections
► Consultation with legal counsel and financial advisers as needed
► Review of shareholder reports
► Monitoring committee activities and recommendations

The duty of loyalty demands that officers and directors act on behalf of your corporation in good faith. Lawsuits alleging breach of this duty usually arise when an officer or director:

► Usurps, for his personal benefit, an opportunity belonging to the corporation (see section 11.05);
► Has a conflict of interest or engages in self-dealing;
► Withdraws excessive compensation from the corporate treasury;
► Employs corporate funds in ways designed to perpetuate personal control over the corporation; or
► Pushes through so-called poison-pill measures that not only prevent take-over bids but also permanently impair the value of shares of corporate stock.

Your two most important defenses against lawsuits alleging failure on your part, or on the part of your other executives, to meet legally imposed duties are the *business judgment rule* and the *reliance defense.*

The business judgment rule protects decisions that you and your other executives make in good faith. The rule holds that directors are not guarantors, that you will not be held accountable for errors of, or mistakes in, judgment, and that you are at least entitled to an initial presumption that your decisions are properly based on sufficient information. A person suing any of you, thus, is required to rebut the initial presumption of propriety.

Obviously, you and your executives are better equipped than the courts to make day-to-day decisions concerning your regular business affairs. Usually, a court does not consider itself qualified to intervene in the decision-making processes of a corporation unless it has been shown that an executive has a conflict of interest or has breached a duty of loyalty to the corporation.

As for the reliance defense, most state corporation laws provide that you and your directors are entitled to rely on certain information, opinions, reports, or statements (including financial statements and other financial data) that are supplied by others within and outside the corporation.

The primary requirements, in order to be covered by the reliance defense, are that the information or statements were prepared or presented by corporate counsel, public accountants, or other qualified persons and that the information or statements related to matters that you had reason to believe were within the provider's professional or expert competence.

Some requirements for the reliance defense relate specifically to where the advice of an attorney is involved. In such a case, you would need to show that you:

► Made complete disclosure to counsel
► Sought the attorney's advice in regard to the legality of a contemplated action
► Received advice that was legal
► Relied in good faith on that advice.

However, you may not argue the defense if:

► You knew all pertinent facts were not disclosed to counsel;
► You knew the attorney's advice was contrary to law;
► You knew the attorney or other expert was not competent to advise you on the particular matter;
► You had knowledge of the attorney's conflict of interest or bad faith;
► You did not specifically follow the advice rendered; or
► The good-faith requirement was not satisfied for some other reason.

In addition to that of attorneys, most state laws permit you to rely on other information or advice, or both, as follows:

► The books of account or reports made to the corporation by any of its officials;

► Financial statements, reports, or other materials or information obtained from an independent certified public accountant;

► Evaluations of an appraiser selected with reasonable care by the board of directors or by a committee of the board; or

► Other records of the corporation prepared or obtained in good faith.

Although the reliance defense is permitted to corporate officers as well as to directors, officers as a group are expected to be more familiar with a corporation's affairs than are its directors. Thus, an officer may be held as not entitled to rely on certain information, such as sales or earnings reports with which he is closely familiar, in a situation where a director could safely assume the correctness of the documents. Since personal liabilities can also be imposed on executives for misrepresenting corporate information, they should be aware of the circumstances in which such liability often arises, as set forth in Exhibit 11-3.

You can take certain further steps to protect yourself from accusations that you failed to meet your duties of care and loyalty. At a minimum, you should take into account the following points for your corporate risk-reduction program:

Exhibit 11-3. Checklist of circumstances in which personal liability has been imposed for misrepresentation of corporate information.

☐ An executive falsely represented a material fact concerning the corporation's business, activities, or affairs.

☐ The executive knew that the representation was false (or knew the representation was recklessly made without reasonable grounds to believe it was true).

☐ The misrepresentation was made with the intent to induce another party to act on it.

☐ The other party acted or restrained from action in reliance on the representation.

☐ The other party suffered damage as a result of such reliance.

---

1. Financial statements on the internal operations of your company should be prepared regularly and made available to officers and directors in such a way that the materials can be readily understood.

2. You and your other executives should from time to time be given reports that deal with compliance in matters that materially affect your business (e.g., securities, environmental and antitrust areas).

3. You and your executives should be made aware of the day-to-day activities of the company, including current and future planning, potential problems that confront the company, and new areas into which it is venturing.

4. Lengthy, written reports are not required and usually are not the most effective method for corporate personnel to communicate information to directors. Instead, one or more executives can update the directors informally at the beginning of board meetings. The discussion should include questions and viewpoints from the directors.

5. Elaboration of company policy on common liability areas, such as conflicts of interest and self-dealing, should be communicated to officers and directors in order to make it clear what the potential sources of liability are and to what extent the company will back them up.

6. Directors and officers should be aware of the extent of disclosure required in company reports and other releases to the public (see section 11.06).

7. Corporate legal counsel should attend all board meetings so that directors can obtain legal opinions as decisions are being made. In addition, corporate counsel should periodically make officers and directors aware of liability developments, current cases, and laws that may affect corporate decisions and policies.

8. Legal counsel should be aware of personal conflict that may result from serving as a director or officer of your corporation while serving as the company's attorney.

9. In addition to having an independent auditor, a committee within the company can be involved with financial audits. That committee can review the opinions and suggestions of the outside auditor and make audit information available to the directors as a group. It may be beneficial for the directors on the audit committee to meet with the auditor without company personnel being present so that both sides can be completely candid with each other.

11.05 Conflict of Interest and Corporate Opportunity

The duty of loyalty is treated generally in section 11.04, but two subsidiary duties in relation to *conflict of interest* and *corporate opportunity* require separate treatment in order to provide a full explanation.

You and your executives can be held personally liable for engaging in a transaction constituting a conflict of interest between your personal interest and that of the corporation. The so-called corporate opportunity doctrine is the most common application of the conflict of interest rule, but other examples of such conflict arise in cases such as these:

- ► An officer or director purchases corporate assets on terms very favorable to him.
- ► An officer or director enters into a leasing agreement with your corporation on terms personally favorable.
- ► An executive with a personal interest votes for the adoption of, or is otherwise actively involved in the adoption of, a compensation, retirement, insurance, or fringe benefit plan or perquisite or other arrangement.
- ► An executive sells or leases assets to the corporation for a favorable price or rent.

The corporate opportunity doctrine prohibits you and other officers and directors, and the shareholders if you have a closely held (fewer than thirty-five shareholders) corporation, from personally acquiring an opportunity that would have been valuable to the corporation's business, unless the opportunity is first offered to the corporation and is declined by a disinterested or nondominated board of directors.

The size of a corporation is not normally relevant when considering the corporate opportunity doctrine. However, although shareholders normally do not have a duty of loyalty, it has been held that shareholders of a close corporation owe to each other a duty in the operation of their corporation similar to the duty that partners owe to one another—that duty being, in effect, a variation of the corporate opportunity doctrine. Thus, in order for shareholders of a close corporation to take advantage of an opportunity deemed corporate, they may need to obtain implicit or explicit consent from the other shareholders if they wish to avoid personal liability.

The corporate opportunity doctrine will be applied to your business when reasons of fairness suggest that it should be applied. For example:

▶ Whether a particular business opportunity is one in which your corporation has an expectancy growing out of an existing contractual right.

▶ Whether there is a specially advantageous relationship between the opportunity and your corporation's business plans, purposes, or current activities.

▶ Whether the opportunity involves activities adaptable to your business and into which your corporation might easily expand.

▶ Whether there is a competitive nature to the opportunity and compatibility with other lines of goods or services sold by your company.

▶ Whether your corporation has the ability to acquire the opportunity as a financial, economic, or legal matter. For example, if your business does not have the capabilities of entering into certain areas of production, or if it lacks the financial ability to expand current operations, then the doctrine would probably not be applicable.

▶ Whether the use of corporate assets to acquire the opportunity would be detrimental, or advantageous, to the corporation in view of other current operations.

▶ Whether the opportunity includes activities about which your corporation has fundamental knowledge, practical experience, facilities, equipment, personnel, and the ability to pursue.

▶ The extent to which your corporation needs to take advantage of an opportunity in order to remain a continuing business, or whether the opportunity is essential to satisfy an existing goal of your business.

▶ Whether your corporation under its certificate of incorporation, or through action by the board or its shareholders, has declared that it is interested in taking advantage of specific types of business opportunities.

▶ Whether the existence of the opportunity was communicated to executives in a covert or suspicious manner.

▶ Whether you or another executive, on learning of the opportunity, relayed information about it in a full and forthright manner to others involved.

▶ Whether you or other officers or directors, on learning about the opportunity, took action indicating a substantial amount of interest.

You will not be held liable for the appropriation of a business opportunity if it is determined not to be a corporate opportunity and there is no evidence of fraud or breach of duty. In addition, even where the opportunity is deemed a corporate one, liability will not be imposed if you can establish that the channeling of the opportunity in a direction other than to the corporation did not violate the duty of loyalty or constitute bad faith or unfair dealing.

11.06 Liabilities Under the Securities Acts

Your most significant areas of potential personal liability under federal and state securities laws are as follows:

▶ Liability for selling *unregistered securities*, such as stocks or bonds not covered by a document required to be filed with a government agency at the time of issuance.

▶ Liability for misstatements or omissions in a *registration statement,* which is the document required to be filed with a government agency at the time of issuing securities.

▶ Liability for *short-swing profits*—gains obtained by both buying and selling, within the same six-month period, one or more registered securities issued by the corporation—and liability for failure to file a report with the appropriate government agency regarding any purchase or sale of a registered security of the company.

▶ Liability for selling a security by means of a material misrepresentation or omission.

Although criminal liability is possible, particularly in cases of deliberate fraud, the usual risk exposure you have under the securities laws is to a judgment awarding of civil damages to a person or the corporation incurring loss as a result of a violation of the particular statutory provision, together with legal fees and costs.

As a major shareholder in a small business, a common type of lawsuit for you to encounter is one alleging that you bought or sold stock or another security of the company on the basis of *inside information.* Inside information is any private data that can materially affect the value of a security, such as knowledge of the price that some party is willing to pay for shares, whether or not an actual offer has been made.

When a minority shareholder is induced to sell his stock on the basis of material misrepresentations, he may be in a position to recover damages from the seller of controlling interest under state law—the common law of fraud—but the more typical case is brought under Section 10(b) of the Securities Exchange Act of 1934 and Rule 10b-5 of the Securities and Exchange Commission (SEC). Where you as the majority shareholder purchase stock on the open market with the intent to resell that stock on the basis of, or following disclosure of, inside information, the important question is whether or not you had an affirmative duty to make public disclosure prior to completing the purchase. Rule 10b-5 states:

> It shall be unlawful for any person, directly or indirectly, by the use of any means or instrumentality of interstate commerce, or of the mails or of any facility of any national securities exchange,

(a) To employ any device, scheme, or artifice to defraud,
(b) To make any untrue statement of a material fact or to omit to state a material fact necessary in order to make the statements made, in the light of the circumstances under which they were made not misleading, or
(c) To engage in any act, practice, or course of business which operates or would operate as a fraud or deceit upon any person, in connection with the purchase of any security.

Although nondisclosure of material private information prior to buying or selling a corporate security is clearly risky, there are circumstances under which you may be able to avoid liability, such as these:

▶ Where your sale or purchase is made through a broker or on an organized stock exchange;
▶ Where your nondisclosure is of opinion, not fact; or
▶ Where the other party conducts an independent investigation and acts in reliance thereon.

There are five requirements for liability under the common law of fraud, as follows:

1. A material fact was falsely represented;
2. The party representing the fact knew that the statement was false (or the representation was recklessly made without reasonable grounds to believe it was true);
3. The misrepresentation was made with the intent to induce the party to act on such information;
4. The party acted or restrained from action in reliance on the representation; and
5. The party suffered damage as a result of such reliance.

A highly sensitive area for you and other executives of small corporations is the handling of disclosure of a *tender offer*, or an offer made to buy a controlling interest in your company. Consideration of federal securities disclosure requirements is the first step, starting with *Rule 14e-2* of the Securities Exchange Act of 1934.

Rule 14e-2 requires a *target* corporation, or the company for which an offer is made, within ten days after such offer, to send its securities holders a statement recommending acceptance or rejection of the tender offer and indicating neutrality or inability to take a position with respect to the tender offer. The statement of management's position must give reasons for the recommendation, neutrality, or failure to take a position.

The target company's recommendation is required to meet further specified disclosure requirements if the tender offer is for registered equity securities. In such instances, the target company must file a *Schedule 14d-9* with the SEC and give the offeror a copy. Schedule 14d-9 must include the reasons for management's particular recommendation, a description of any material agreement or understanding, any real or potential conflict of interest between the target and the offeror, and a statement on whether or not negotiations are under way as a response to the tender offer.

Such negotiations may relate to a:

► Merger;
► Reorganization;
► Purchase, sale, or transfer of the target company's assets;
► Tender offer for the target's stock;
► Material change in capital of the corporation; or
► Material change in corporate dividend policy.

Section 14(e) of the Securities Exchange Act of 1934 prohibits material misrepresentations or omissions as well as "fraudulent, deceptive or manipulative acts or practices" in association with tender offers or solicitation of securities holders in support of or in opposition to such offers. The term "tender offer" is not defined by Section 14(e). The target corporation and its directors are subject to the provisions of Section 14(e) with respect to all communications to shareholders encouraging the acceptance or rejection of a particular tender offer.

If you sell *unregistered* securities for your personal account, you will violate Section 5 of the Securities Act of 1933. You need not have any direct dealing with the buyer, or *privity,* in view of Section 12(1) of the Act. If, however, your corporation is the seller of securities, your personal liability, in the absence of *control* liability, depends upon whether you participated in the sale in a meaningful way—just signing the stock certificates is not enough. However, if you own an amount of the company stock substantial enough to constitute "control" or if you otherwise play a major role in your company's sale of unregistered securities, you may find yourself liable personally for the violation of Section 5.

If your company does register and sell securities, you may be able to protect against accusations of misrepresentations or omissions under the *due diligence* defense. The term "due diligence" generally means "making a reasonable investigation." Potentially, you may, as to the accuracy of the information contained in the general, or "unexpertised" portion of a registration statement, be held liable as if you were a guarantor of that data. However, if you did not have actual knowledge of all relevant facts, you should be able to establish due diligence on the basis of a reasonable investigation of company affairs.

The due diligence defense also applies to other categories of participants in the sale of registered securities, such as:

▶ Outside directors
▶ Lawyers and accountants
▶ Underwriters
▶ Appraisers and other experts

Another area of potential liability that you should consider under the securities laws is that of *selling control*. If you sell stock or other interests that represent control of your company, a court may impose certain duties to minority shareholders and the corporation. Control might exist even though you own less than 50 percent of the shares, depending on the size of your corporation, the number of shareholders, and concentration of ownership. Generally, you do have control if you can direct or cause the direction of the management and policies of the corporation.

As an example of selling control, suppose you were able to sell a third or so of your company's stock by agreeing to obtain the resignations of a majority of the directors and replace them with the buyer's nominees. You could be held liable to minority shareholders for the amount of consideration you received for the shares in excess of their market value, often referred to as the premium for the control shares.

Most courts are of the view that a premium, in this sense, belongs to the seller of a majority interest because it is inherent in the stock ownership. Under this view, a majority shareholder may sell his stock at the most advantageous price possible without the necessity to share any premium gained with either the corporation or the minority shareholders.

Other courts, which are in a minority, hold that the power to direct the affairs of a corporation is a corporate asset and that the premium for such an asset belongs either to the corporation's treasury or to all the shareholders on a pro rata basis.

11.07 Statutory Limitations on Liability

Most states have enacted new types of limitations on the personal liabilities of corporate directors, which apply in some instances to officers as well. These statutes take various forms and provide different applications and exceptions that warrant your consideration if you are about to incorporate or are interested in gaining protection by reincorporating in another state.

Delaware has long had the most popular corporation statute. This law was changed in 1987 to provide that while a certificate of incorporation may purport to eliminate or limit the liability of directors to their corporation or to shareholders for breach of "fiduciary duty," there are four exceptions, and a certificate of incorporation may not limit potential liabilities:

- ▸ For breach of a director's duty of loyalty;
- ▸ For acts or omissions not in good faith or involving intentional misconduct or knowing violation of law;
- ▸ For willful or negligent conduct in paying dividends or repurchasing stock out of other than lawfully available funds; or
- ▸ For any transaction from which a director derives an improper personal benefit.

Even if you have already incorporated, it would be advisable to check with your attorney about the possibility of reincorporating in a state that extends greater protection against personal liability for corporate executives than does your current state of incorporation.

Certainly if you have not yet incorporated, this is a subject you and your lawyer should consider at length. Selecting a state law that provides the greatest overall relief from personal liability largely depends on the risk exposures that weigh heaviest in your particular situation.

11.08 D&O Insurance

At the time you incorporate, and from time to time thereafter, you should consider carefully *director and officer* (D&O) insurance. Under the typical D&O policy, you have two separate insureds, the corporation and its executives. Your corporation is not insured against its own wrongdoing; rather, it is insured to the extent that it indemnifies or is required to indemnify your executives for claims made against them for their own wrongdoing (see section 11.09).

The limited number of companies that continue to write D&O policies rely heavily on new policy exclusions to limit underwriting risks. As recently as 1983, the typical D&O policy excluded from coverage only claims for libel and slander, personal injuries, short-swing profits from insider trading, remuneration paid without necessary board approval, the unlawful gain of personal profit or advantage, and such wrongful acts determined by a court to be actively and deliberately dishonest. On the whole, those exclusions left a great deal of coverage in place. (The last two exclusions referred to were designed to avoid duplication of the coverage provided by blanket bonds.)

The exclusions in D&O policies raise the question of what coverage remains. The most common new exclusions apply to litigation brought by regulatory agencies, suits brought by shareholders, suits brought by the corporation itself, suits based on acts occurring prior to the commencement of the policy period, and legal action resulting from board decisions made to fend off a hostile takeover. By any account, the new provisions have resulted in a substantial decrease in coverage.

D&O policies directly insure officers and directors for their *wrongful acts* that result in a *loss*. A wrongful act is usually defined as an act, error, omission, neglect, or misleading statement made by an officer or director in his management capacity as such and in the discharge of corporate duties, or claims made against an officer or director solely because of his position. "Loss" is usually defined as moneys that officers and directors become legally obliged to pay as a result of claims asserted against them because of alleged wrongful acts, including legal fees, other defense costs, judgments, and settlement payments to which the insurer has consented.

The single most important feature of D&O policies from your company's standpoint may be that they are usually written on a *claims made* basis rather than on an *occurrence* basis. This means that coverage is provided only for claims that are deemed to have been "made" during the policy period. Thus, even if a wrongful act occurs during the policy period, coverage is usually denied unless a claim based on the act is actually made to the insurer during the policy period.

A claim is made by providing the insurer with written notice. The most obvious circumstance in which a claim is deemed to have been made during the policy period is where an officer or director is either sued or threatened with suit and the insurer is provided with written notice of such during the policy period.

A sometimes more important, and less obvious, way to make a claim under a D&O policy is to send the insurer written notice of an "occurrence" that, although not presently the basis of a threatened or asserted suit, might in the future give rise to a suit being brought for an alleged wrongful act. A notice of such a potential claim may allow you or your other executives who believe they have acted or failed to act in a way that might expose them to litigation to "lock in" their policy rights by providing notice to the insurer during the policy period of the occurrence creating that exposure. In doing so, you will establish your rights under the policy, and any benefits afforded under the policy will be available even if you are not sued until years after the policy period expires.

Since D&O insurance is difficult to secure these days, it may not be a good idea to flood the insurer with notices of every conceivable act, omission, or event that could possibly precipitate a suit, especially if the likelihood of a lawsuit is remote or if the potential exposure does not greatly exceed the policy's deductible amount.

Corporate blanket bonds are different from D&O policies. The former insure "dishonest acts," whereas the latter expressly exclude "acts of active and deliberate dishonesty." In theory, a loss covered by the blanket bond is by definition excluded from coverage by the dishonesty exclusion of the D&O policy.

If you have a blanket bond on executives, it may be practical for you to control your claims exposure by circulating a due diligence questionnaire to your bonded employees. The questionnaire should inquire in detail about actual, threatened, or potential claims. If a claim is not discovered because an employee has withheld information, you may still have a valid bond claim for loss sustained by reason of the employee's failure to honestly answer the questionnaire. Also, the exercise of due diligence through the use of a questionnaire may eliminate future arguments by the insurance company that your application for the policy was not completed truthfully to the extent of your own knowledge.

An officer or director who is terminated or otherwise leaves office should, with the aid of a lawyer, carefully review all applicable insurance coverages, especially if the termination is based on allegations of negligent performance of duties. Many former officers and directors have found themselves defendants in suits brought by shareholders or by the corporation long after they have left its employ, and have found that coverage under the D&O policy in effect during their employment has expired.

When a sale or other change in control occurs, it is particularly advisable for you to be sensitive to insurance issues. It sometimes happens that the purchaser of a corporation attempts to recoup part of the purchase price through a negligence suit against the seller. You should also review your indemnification bylaws (section 11.09) to be sure that they are, and will remain, mandatory to the extent permitted by law.

11.09   Indemnification

Your corporation should have bylaw provisions for your *indemnification* and that of any key executives to the fullest extent permitted by statute. To indemnify someone is to hold him harmless against loss, liability, or expense in a particular situation. The bylaws should make it clear that litigation expenses will be advanced when and as they are incurred, assuming the *indemnitee*—the person covered by the indemnity—executes an agreement to reimburse the advances if he is ultimately held not entitled to indemnification. Under the law of several states, indemnification is mandatory in many situations.

While most corporate expenses in indemnifying executives are deductible for tax purposes, the deduction cannot be taken for amounts used to pay fines or penalties. However, the legal expenses in defending against criminal liability, even if the case is lost, are still deductible. Although some of the indemnity and D&O insurance (section 11.08) benefits may seem to be personal rather than corporate, the IRS has ruled that indemnification expenses and D&O premiums may be claimed as trade or business expenses or as employee fringe benefits—additional compensation expense. However, if the latter method of claiming the deduction is used, then the recipient executives are limited by a 2 percent ceiling on the amount of their miscellaneous deductions. Thus, the business expense type of deduction is more practical in most situations than the additional compensation expense deduction.

11.10   The Insecurity of Protection

The need to gain protection for you and your executives is undeniable, but a law of diminishing returns clearly applies to your efforts in that direction. By the time this book finds its fullest circulation, D&O insurance may simply not be available from any reputable company. The possibility of reincorporating in a jurisdiction that offers more protection in some areas may be far outweighed by additional taxes or open or hidden costs of being incorporated outside the principal state where you do business—clearly you would need to qualify as a foreign corporation in the states where you do business. Notwithstanding the limitations, it will in any event be advantageous for you to avail yourself to some extent of the benefits of your corporate risk-reduction program.

12 Looking Ahead

Tomorrow is a new day; you shall begin it well and serenely and with high spirit.

              —Ralph Waldo Emerson

12.01   Debt vs. Equity

The successful are never content to stagnate, and so it is that you will eventually begin to look for large infusions of new capital to increase your company's productivity. Yet the attraction of capital can be costly and even risky. Consider, for example, the relative merits of the financing technique described in the following sections.

▶ *Debt.* Debt financing is especially appealing to the prosperous corporation. Its cost—interest—is tax deductible at the corporate level, and although debt holders can impose controls, no dilution of ownership is suffered. For the investor, debt is the safest of all securities and offers tax-free recovery of investment, along with a "guaranteed" fixed rate of return.

Debt has many faces: short-term bank loans, leases and sale-leasebacks, mortgages, long-term private placements, debentures secured by the company's general credit, and bonds secured by specific assets. Each has its own rewards and drawbacks for both the business and the investor.

▶ *Equity.* Equity financing means the sale of an ownership interest, and with it, a reduction in control. It also means the payment of dividends in expensive after-tax dollars.

On the other hand, equity financing can bring in tax-free capital without imposing a fixed obligation on your company—and that looks truly impressive on the financial statement. Equity financing comes in various forms, each with different consequences.

215

Common stock offers the investor great volatility along with great potential for capital appreciation. The holder of common stock—last in line at liquidation—has the right to vote along with you and to share with you any increase or decrease in earnings and the underlying value of your company.

Theoretically at least, *preferred stock* is more conservative. The holder of preferred stock has a claim to dividends and assets upon liquidation that is superior to the claim of the holder of common stock. Preferred shares vary as far as rights are concerned: They may be voting shares; they may be *cumulative*, requiring your company to make up any dividends in arrears; they may be *callable*, redeemable by your company at a set price; or they may be *participating*, entitling the holder to share in any dividends beyond a specified floor.

▶ *Combos*. Imaginative lawyers have combined the advantages of debt and equity financing, and these combinations may provide the easiest way to attract investors. Debentures or preferred stock, for instance, may be convertible into common stock; the investor assumes a small front-end risk but may later share in capital gain. Your company, however, must tackle the tricky task of setting a conversion price low enough to attract investors and high enough to circumvent a gross dilution.

Rights, options, and warrants serve the same purpose—to offer the investor a relatively low-risk opportunity that just might appreciate in the years to come. Finally, packages of debt and equity can help the investor hedge his bet.

12.02 Seven Good Creditors

The issuance of debt is often thought to be the most desirable trade-off for investment capital, for, along with its other virtues, it presupposes your continuing and exclusive ownership of your business. Luckily, all kinds of pure-debt opportunities may be yours for the asking:

1. Commercial banks offer letters of credit and short- and intermediate-term loans (see section 7.04).

2. The federal government offers SBA loans, EDA loans, MBDA loans, and many others. The Economic Development Administration (EDA), an agency of the Department of Commerce, provides business development loans to assist economically deprived areas. The Minority Business Development Agency (MBDA), another Commerce Department agency, provides business development loans to minority businesses.
3. State and local governments offer development loans.
4. Equipment manufacturers and leasing companies offer leases and sale-leasebacks, which are often desirable off-balance-sheet financing methods.
5. Factors finance receivables.
6. Trade suppliers may offer both credit and side loans.
7. Even tax-exempt organizations may offer grants and loans to certain select industries.

12.03   Sharing the Wealth

Once pure debt opportunities have been exhausted, your options narrow, and those who want to share in your equity become logical candidates. These are a few to consider:

▶ *Insiders.* No doubt you will have already tapped your own bank account, but don't overlook the people who work for you. Stock options (section 10.01 on "Shares") and ESOPs (section 10.03 on "Variations"), to name two vehicles, can serve to reinvest employee-compensation expense in your future growth.

An ESOP financing is a derivative of the qualified stock bonus plan, employing leveraging. Simply stated, the ESOP-leveraging technique involves the sale by the employer company (or majority shareholders) of company stock to an ESOP trust for cash; the trust borrows the purchase price from a bank, insurance company, or mutual fund, using the stock as collateral; and the employer contributes an amount to the trust each year sufficient to repay the loan and interest. The annual contributions to the trust are effectively tax-deductible payments of principal and interest. Future appreciation in the value of the stock held by the trust is shared by plan participants, and the lender is allowed to exclude 50 percent of the interest it earns from its taxable income.

ESOPs can leverage the purchase of another company, refinance existing debt, create a market for corporate stock, transfer control to key personnel upon the founder's retirement, or purchase life insurance with pre-tax dollars, but a lending bank, insurance company, or mutual fund obtains the 50 percent interest exclusion only on loans used to purchase company stock.

For many years, an estate could sell company stock to an ESOP and exclude 50 percent of the sale proceeds from the taxable estate of the seller, but that provision was limited as to sales after February 26, 1987, so that the maximum reduction in estate taxes through this type of transaction is currently $750,000; other restrictions also apply. However, by complying with the restrictions, it is still possible to reduce estate taxes by up to the $750,000 maximum through such a sale—not a small amount for many shareholders in small businesses.

▶ *Private venture-capital firms.* These use their own resources to invest in closely held enterprises that offer long-term big returns. Some prominent venture capitalists are Greylock Management Corp. (Boston), Mesirow Venture Capital (Chicago), Enterprise Capital Corp. (Houston, Texas), Ivanhoe Venture Capital (La Jolla, California), Freshstart Venture Capital Corp. (New York), South Atlantic Venture Fund (Tampa Bay, Florida), and EG&G, Inc. (Wellesley, Massachusetts).

▶ *Venture-capital subsidiaries.* Large, diversified corporations provide capital to companies they intend to acquire at a later date.

▶ *Small business investment companies (SBICs).* These have access to SBA money and get preferential tax treatment. They can take big risks to realize high interest on their debt position as well as the right to purchase equity. A word of warning: SBICs expect the right to major equity participation through conversion or separate warrants, and they impose strict controls (see section 7.04).

▶ *Pension funds.* Pension funds have lots of money, but they cannot speculate.

▶ *Insurance companies.* Same as pension funds.

▶ *The public.* As we will see, this can be the biggest and best source of all.

▶ *Your competition.* A competitor would seem to be the worst source, but sometimes a minority partnership position for your competitor can be negotiated as a way to obtain needed funds on terms better than those you could get from an institutional participant.

12.04   Why Merge?

Sharing your equity with others may be a fair exchange when they share their equity with you. More often than you might expect, unrelenting profits trigger the need to accelerate growth by acquiring or merging with a competitor, or even by being acquired by one. Expansion spurs expansion. Motives vary, but the following factors are the most frequently cited in buy-ins and sellouts.

- ▶ *Diversification.* A merger or acquisition can enhance overall profitability and creditworthiness. What's more, the introduction of new products and services can help level peaks and valleys in profits and cash flow.
- ▶ *Operating economies.* The combination of similar businesses can effect genuine cost economies, and it may increase the relative output of each employee.
- ▶ *Access to assets.* It is often cheaper and always easier to buy, rather than develop, a new product, contract rights, intellectual property, a competent sales force, and many other tough-to-build assets.
- ▶ *Efficiency.* A company's physical plant and systems will pay for themselves much faster once they are fully used, such as through the addition of new business.
- ▶ *Tax advantages.* Under very strict rules, a buyer can acquire a seller's net operating loss carryover and use a limited part of it to offset taxable income each year.
- ▶ *Internal strife.* A sale or merger may be contemplated by a

solid enterprise that is plagued by interowner dissension, or it may be considered by a less-than-solid enterprise seeking a way out.

▶ *Personal planning.* Retirement or estate planning objectives may require the diversification of personal holdings or the creation of a liquid market for them. A sale or merger can do both.

12.05   A More Perfect Union

Tax law considerations, corporate law considerations, and antitrust law considerations coalesce in the structuring of a merger or acquisiton, so it is one of the most complex of legal transactions. In the broadest terms, there are three approaches worth examining:

Asset Acquisition
A buyer may purchase all or part of the seller's assets and business for cash, property, or securities. The seller's stock ownership and corporate structure remain intact until the seller corporation is liquidated and the net sales proceeds are distributed to its shareholders.

Pros	Cons
▶ Minority interests may be bypassed. Minority shareholders will usually have no veto but merely the right to be bought out, and rarely will they have a right of appraisal.	▶ An asset acquisition can be expensive: Title to each asset must be separately transferred.
▶ Typically, the buyer's shareholders will not need to approve an asset acquisition.	▶ Third-party consents are often required to transfer contracts, leases, and licenses.
▶ The buyer will not assume the seller's undisclosed liabilities, or any liabilities it does not agree to assume.	▶ Any of the seller's long-term debt that restricts a sale of assets may need to be recast.
▶ A purchase price allocation	▶ Compliance under bulk-sales laws—protecting creditors against a debtor's selling of its business and abscond-

can offer substantial tax savings.

ing with the proceeds—will be required.

▶ If buyer's securities serve as consideration, the transaction may later be viewed as a merger, voidable without proper notice to shareholders.

Stock Acquisition

The seller's shareholders sell all or part of their stock for cash, property, or the buyer's securities. Since the seller corporation is not a party to the transaction (but its shareholders are), the seller's management need not approve. When it does not, the acquisition is called a takeover bid.

Pros	Cons
▶ The transaction can be simple, quick, and clean. The only documents that must be delivered are properly endorsed stock certificates.	▶ The seller corporation retains its liabilities. Minority shareholders can hold out and retain a position in the seller corporation.
▶ No third-party approval need be obtained, since the corporation remains as before. Only the shareholders are new.	▶ The purchase price cannot be allocated to specific assets to create a tax advantage for the buyer or seller. Also, the buyer may be taxed on any depreciation recapture or investment-credit recapture on the seller's assets.
▶ No directors' approval is required by the selling corporation.	
▶ The buyer does not directly assume corporate liabilities.	▶ SEC registration may be required if the selling corporation has more than a few shareholders.
▶ Installment income reporting may be available to a seller seeking to defer taxation if there is no established market for the seller's stock.	

Statutory Merger

A statutory merger is the combination of two corporations under a state's corporation laws. After both boards of directors and at least two thirds of the shareholders of each corporation approve the merger, one survives, succeeding by operation of law to the assets and liabilities of the other. The disappearing corporation's shareholders exchange their shares for an equity position in the survivor. A *statutory consolidation* differs only in that both consolidating corporations disappear in favor of a new entity, which issues its stock in exchange for the shares of its predecessors.

Pros	Cons
▶ Title to assets transfers automatically upon compliance with state formalities.	▶ The survivor in a merger—or the consolidated new entity—assumes the obligations of any disappearing corporation.
▶ Dissenting minority shareholders can be bought out for cash, and the buyer can be assured of acquiring full ownership.	▶ The process can be slow and expensive: Shareholders meetings, sometimes with proxy materials and notices, must be conducted.
▶ A wide range of securities may be issued without jeopardizing tax-free treatment.	▶ Two thirds approval of shareholders is generally required by statute, and stubborn dissenters may promote a big cash drain.
▶ Since either entity can survive a merger, nontransferable assets can easily be preserved.	▶ The transaction must conform to state law, which may be limiting.
▶ Required shareholders meetings provide an opportunity to amend the charter and bylaws for the special purposes of the ongoing enterprise.	

12.06   Tax Angles and Pooling-of-Interests Accounting

However the transaction is to be structured, price must be its cornerstone. Whether you determine price on the basis of book value, an independent appraisal, comparable price/earnings ratios within the seller's industry, or otherwise, the method of payment will, of course, significantly affect the net dollar result for both buyer and seller. A taxable acquisition, for example, gives the buyer a new basis in the stock for assets purchased, and the seller must recognize its own gain or loss. A "tax-free" acquisition transfers the seller's basis in its stock or assets to the buyer and postpones taxation of the seller's gain or loss until the seller disposes of the securities received in payment.

Tax-free reorganizations include: *A-type consolidation or merger*, which complies with state law and meets Internal Revenue Code standards; *B-type stock acquisition*, in which the seller corporation exchanges at least 80 percent of its voting stock (and no other security) for voting stock of the buyer corporation (and no other security, property, or cash); and *C-type asset acquisition*, in which the buyer corporation acquires substantially all the assets of the seller corporation in exchange for the buyer's voting stock (and possibly a limited amount of other consideration).

Reorganization rules are tricky, but these three basics must always be demonstrated:

1. There must be a continuity of interest, so the sellers must be paid in the stock of the buying corporation, and they must hold it.
2. There must be a continuity of business enterprise, meaning only that the acquired business must continue to operate.
3. There must be a nontax business purpose, so tax avoidance may not be a central reason for the reorganization.

A major nontax consideration in most mergers and acquisitions is that of accounting for the ongoing business under the *pooling-of-interests* accounting method. In a pooling of interests, the buyer's and seller's assets, liabilities, and surpluses or deficits are aggregated. No new goodwill item is entered on the buyer's books where the price exceeds the book value of the seller's assets, and no write-off is made against the buyer's after-tax earnings. The buyer can stay profit pretty, but only if the requirements for the pooling-of-interests accounting method are met. If those requirements are not met, the purchase method is used, under which there will be write-offs against future earnings to amortize the amount by which the purchase price exceeds the book value of the acquired company. The requirements for the pooling-of-interests method are set out in Exhibit 12-1.

12.07   Issues Worth Negotiating

Taxable or tax free, a merger or acquisition invariably raises such diverse issues that setting a price and agreeing to a general structure are only the first skirmish in an intense bargaining campaign. You will spot these issues—and their resolution—in the acquisition contract your lawyer prepares for signature.

Seller's Representations

The seller will warrant the legal status of its stock and the condition of its business as described in appended financial statements. In a stock-for-stock transaction, the shareholders will, of course, warrant their title to the shares they are selling.

Other warranties might include the ownership of the seller's assets and the physical condition of tangibles; the status of lawsuits and actions by government agencies, including the IRS; and in a stock-for-stock transaction, the seller's investment purpose in acquiring the buyer's shares.

An investment-purpose warranty will help avoid the registration requirement under the Securities Act of 1933, and it will ensure continuity of equity ownership for pooling-of-interests purposes.

Buyer's Representations

Where the buyer is paying the seller in stock, the buyer will warrant that its stock is authorized and issued, fully paid and non-assessable.

Assets

The description of stock will be simple, but other assets may be difficult to define, and the purchase of assets demands an allocation

Exhibit 12-1. Requirements for using the pooling-of-interests accounting method following a merger or consolidation ("combination").

1 **One planned transaction.** The combination must be effectuated in one transaction or within twelve months according to a specific plan.

2 **Independence.** The companies must have been independent, and neither must have been a subsidiary of the other during the preceding two years.

3 **Common stock solely.** Only common stock with the same rights as those of the majority of voting common stock outstanding may be issued in exchange for 90% or more of the voting common stock of another corporation.

4 **Maintenance of voting interest.** Both companies must maintain substantially the same voting common stock interest after the combination as before.

5 **Relative stock interests.** Stock must be issued pro rata, and the relative interests of the shareholders must be maintained.

6 **Acquisition of own shares.** Each company may acquire only a limited quantity of its own stock for purposes not related to the combination—e.g., for an ESOP on a regular purchasing basis.

7 **Exercise of voting rights.** Voting rights in the resulting corporation may be exercisable only by the shareholders themselves.

8 **Contingencies.** The plan of combination may not, with few exceptions, provide for issuance of stock or other securities or consideration on a contingent basis.

9 **Postcombination stock purchases.** There cannot be an arrangement that the resulting corporation will acquire any shares issued under the plan.

10 **Former shareholders.** Except for deferred compensation plans and stock options, former shareholders must not be provided for under any ongoing financial arrangements.

11 **Significant liquidations.** There cannot be a plan or arrangement to liquidate any significant part of the assets of the two companies within two years after the combination, except as necessary to eliminate duplicate or excess assets or as would otherwise occur in the ordinary course of the resulting company's business.

12 **Reporting earnings.** The earnings of the acquired company prior to the combination may not be included in reports of earnings of the resulting company.

13 **Costs of pooling.** The costs of pooling may not be charged against capital surplus.

14 **Partial pooling.** Partial pooling is not permitted.

of the purchase to fix tax consequences (see Exhibit 12-1 and IRS Form 8594).

Purchase Price
The price may be a predetermined dollar amount or number of shares; or a formula may be adopted, setting the price as a function of the seller's future earnings or some other variable.

Assumption of Liabilities
A stock purchase necessitates the assumption of all corporate liabilities; after all, there will be no change in the corporation's identity. A sale of assets, on the other hand, may or may not be accompanied by the buyer's assumption of certain of the seller's liabilities.

Seller's Indemnification
The seller will typically indemnify the buyer against any unassumed liabilities in an assets purchase, and the seller's indemnification may be secured by a pledge of stock.

Antitrust Provisions
Any past violation of the antitrust laws by the seller presents an assumption-of-liability question. And the antitrust laws are so sweeping that the seller's consistent compliance should be of real concern to the buyer: The Sherman Act prohibits combinations in restraint of trade—through such activities as price-fixing, territorial divisions, and boycotts—and monopolies of commerce; the Federal Trade Commission Act prohibits unfair methods of competition and unfair or deceptive acts in commerce; and the Robinson-Patman Act prohibits price discrimination injurious to competition.

The acquisition itself may be in violation of the Clayton Act, which prohibits any corporation from acquiring another when the effect of the acquisition may be to lessen competition substantially or to tend to create a monopoly. The language of the Clayton Act has been broadly construed to apply not only to "vertical" combinations of competitors but also to "horizontal" combinations of companies with a buyer-seller relationship (such as a wholesaler and a retailer) and to conglomerates—combinations of companies that sell noncompetitive but related or similar products to different markets. The Act is violated whenever a merger or acquisition substantially lessens competition within a "line of commerce" (which may mean any product aimed at a target market) in any "section of the country," even a state or two. And a substantial lessening of competition is deemed to have occurred whenever a merger or acquisition notably increases an economic concentration, eliminates a substantial source of supply, eliminates a substantial factor in competition, or produces relationships between buyers and sellers that deprive competitors of a fair chance to compete.

The enforcement of federal antitrust laws is carried out by the Federal Trade Commission (FTC) and the Justice Department, and through litigation in the private sector. For certain large acquisitions, whether of assets or stock, both the FTC and the Antitrust Division of the Justice Department must be given reports of certain information for periods of time before consummating the respective transaction. This preacquisition report requirement applies if two conditions are met: an *economic result condition* and a *size condition*. The economic result condition is met if the acquisition would bring the acquirer's holdings up to more than 15 percent in amount or $15 million in market value of the target company's stock or assets. The size condition is met if the acquirer has at least $100 million of assets or annual sales and the target has at least $10 million of assets or annual sales. The size condition is also met if the respective sizes of the two businesses are in reverse of those just described. If both conditions are met, a mandatory waiting period must run before a transaction is consummated. The waiting period is fifteen days for all-cash tender offers for securities and thirty days for other types of offers, whether or not some cash is included.

Most advisers will recommend against seeking antitrust clearance from the Justice Department. Instead, when the buyer and seller fear that federal or competitor action may be instituted to enjoin their transaction, each may contractually retain the right to bow out gracefully upon information and belief that suit has been filed.

Securities Provisions

The buyer in any acquisition calling for securities as payment is an "issuer" of securities and is obligated to register them with the Securities and Exchange Commission (SEC or the Commission), unless the buyer qualifies for a specific exemption. The kind of registration or the specific exemption the issuer elects will affect the seller's ability to dispose of the securities it receives; only a full registration will allow the seller to liquidate its holdings without a hitch. Because of this increased liquidity, the seller will favor registration; because of the expenses and disclosure requirements registration imposes, the buyer will normally resist it. Should the seller prevail, the acquisition agreement will obligate the buyer to register its stock; should the buyer prevail, the agreement will provide that the buyer's stock certificates shall bear a restrictive legend substantially as follows:

> The shares represented by this certificate have not been registered under the Securities Act of 1933, as amended. The shares have been acquired for investment and may not be sold, offered for sale, or transferred in the absence of an effective registration statement for the shares under the Securities Act of 1933, as amended, or an opinion of counsel to the company that registration is not required under said Act.

If either party is subject to the Securities Act of 1934, detailed proxy material must be furnished to its shareholders before the acquisition is voted upon, and also must be prefiled with the SEC at least ten days before distribution to the shareholders or the public. In a complex transaction, a period of more than the minimum ten days for the SEC prefiling is necessary, as the final proxy materials will need to incorporate all changes recommended by the SEC staff. The proxy regulations specify the form of the blank proxy sent to the shareholders and require inquiries of *street name* security holders regarding the identity of the beneficial owners of the securities so held and the number of such beneficial owners so that additional sets of the proxy materials can be supplied. A street name security holder is a stock brokerage concern that holds stock or other securities in its own name for the account of other real parties in interest. If there is a proxy contest, then additional proxy rules apply.

Whether or not the proxy rules under the Securities Exchange Act of 1934 apply to the transaction, the fraud provisions under the Act have to be reckoned with, including the notorious Rule 10b-5 (see section 11.06). Simply stated, Rule 10b-5 prohibits anyone in the buyer's or seller's camp from taking advantage of inside information or failing to disclose material information. If a tender offer is involved in the transaction, then compliance is required with SEC Regulations 14D and 14E and Rule 14f-1 (see section 11.06).

In a transaction in which you are in effect selling control over your company, a review of cases in your jurisdiction where personal liabilities have been imposed on sellers of control is definitely in order (see section 11.06). Your attorney will most likely advise you on this and the other matters involved in your transaction without any specific requests on your part, but a reminder from you can never hurt.

Federal securities laws, state blue-sky laws, and rules regarding stock exchange disclosure and shareholder approval demand conservative compliance. Where registration is to be avoided, a cautious seller may seek a no-action letter from the SEC. Application may be made to Chief Counsel, Division of Corporate Finance, Securities and Exchange Commission, 450 5th Street, N.W., Washington, D.C. 20549.

Employee Provisions

The acquisition agreement should ensure the retention of key personnel through the assignment and delivery of employment contracts.

Any collective bargaining agreement signed by the seller should be reviewed carefully by the buyer's attorney, since it may be binding upon the buyer as a successor employer, even if it has not been specifically assumed.

The seller's retirement plans should be transferred to the buyer and, ideally, integrated into the buyer's existing benefits program. The buyer may assume liability for any of the seller's outstanding stock options and substitute its own options; or it may assume no liability for outstanding options.

Noncompetitive Agreement

The buyer will seek the seller's assurance that it will not compete in the business the seller is acquiring. The buyer should propose language that does not violate restraint of trade principles, for fear of unenforceability and antitrust repercussions. The seller, of course, will want any covenant to be narrowly drafted so as to permit its normal growth without undue impediment (see Exhibit 9.1).

Conduct Pending the Close

The seller will be called upon to operate its business only in its ordinary course until title is transferred, and will be precluded from otherwise selling any of its assets. Farsighted counsel will allow exceptions for any beneficial capital expenditures known to be in the offing when the agreement is signed.

Conditions Precedent

Both buyer and seller may require certain acts or events to take place before they are legally bound to follow through with the transaction. The buyer, for instance, may first insist on a pooling-of-interests opinion from the SEC and, of course, an accountant's certification. The seller may require an opinion from the buyer's attorney confirming the buyer's corporate structure and validating the buyer's warranties, or it may request a tax-free reorganization ruling from the IRS.

Brokerage

If a broker has participated in the transaction, the party responsible for his fee should indemnify the other from any claim.

Nuts and Bolts

Many other requirements may come to the fore. For example:

▶ There should be compliance with bulk sales laws, or the seller should at least indemnify the buyer from any adverse consequences of noncompliance (see section 1.09).

► The parties should agree on who is liable for any sales and use taxes assessed on account of the acquisition.

► Agreement should be reached about responsibility for the completion of pending customer contracts.

And on and on.

12.08 Private Placements

When a merger or acquisition cannot fill the bill, or when a business combination creates a need for ready cash, the time may be right for a public or private offering. A private placement is any offering or sale of a security (any investment instrument) that is exempt from the expensive registration requirements of the Securities Act of 1933 as a "transaction by an issuer not involving any public offering." Usually a less disruptive move than a merger, a private placement can be a cheaper and faster way to gain outside financing than a conventional public offering, and its timing need not depend on the availability of audited financial statements and the workload of the SEC staff. What's more, a privately held company need make no public disclosure of its private offering.

Nearly all businesses issue securities, and almost all securities are exempt from registration. Thus, private placements account for the vast majority of the securities issued in the United States; yet, ironically, few areas of the law have been more treacherous for lawyers and their business clients. Let this be your primer:

1. Section 5 of the Securities Act of 1933 requires that any security be registered with the SEC before it is offered, sold, or delivered by use of the mails or facilities of interstate commerce, unless an exemption is available.

2. Sections 3(a), 4(2), and 4(6) of the Securities Act of 1933 create exemptions as to *intrastate offerings* and *private offerings*.

3. The intrastate offering exemption applies if the company is incorporated in the state in which offers to sell securities are made,

if the company does a significant portion of its business in such state, and if all of the offerees are residents of the such state. This exemption is regarded as treacherous for two reasons: (1) liability for participating in an unregistered offering may be imposed if an offeree resides out of the state in question, even if that person signs an affidavit confirming residence in the required state; (2) if a purchaser resells one of the securities within a year or two to someone not residing in the required state, the exemption may be lost for the entire issue and personal liability could be imposed on the participants, including directors and officers of the offering company. It may be possible to reduce these potential liabilities by complying with Rule 147, which is a so-called "safe harbor" for ensuring that the intrastate exemption will apply. Rule 147 can be used if (1) the company maintains its principal executive offices in the required state (and is incorporated there); (2) derives 80 percent of its revenues from and maintains 80 percent of its assets within and uses 80 percent of the offering proceeds within such state; and (3) none of the purchasers resells any of the securities to a nonresident for at least nine months after the completion of the offering. The last-mentioned condition for Rule 147 renders even the described harbor less than totally safe, since who can know in advance what some purchaser might do over a nine-month period?

4. There are exemptions for private offerings that fall into different categories, as follows:
    a. A *"Regulation A" offering.* This exemption is available to a company whose offerings do not exceed $1.5 million in one year. However, a short form of registration is required notwithstanding the exemption, and if an offering exceeds $100,000, then an offering circular similar to a prospectus must be prepared and given to each purchaser. Since there is no true exemption under Regulation A, an offering pursuant to its terms is usually called a baby registration (see section 12.10).
    b. A *"Rule 506" offering.* This exemption, which is set out in the SEC's Regulation D, is available if (1) certain sale restrictions are met, (2) prescribed notices are sent to the SEC, and (3) offers or sales are made only to *accredited*

investors plus up to thirty-five other persons who are reasonably believed to have such knowledge and experience in financial and business matters as to be capable of evaluating the merits and risks of the prospective investment; persons reasonably believed to have such capability are generally referred to as sophisticated purchasers. A reasonable belief concerning the required sophistication is presumed if the purchaser is represented by someone who in turn has the necessary evaluation capability. The term "accredited investors" refers to the following:
(1) Individuals who had incomes of over $200,000 in the last two years and reasonably expect such level of income in the current year;
(2) Individuals whose net worth exceeds $1 million;
(3) Persons who purchase $150,000 or more of securities in cash or by means of certain other types of consideration so long as the purchase price does not exceed 20 percent of the purchaser's net worth;
(4) Directors and executive officers of the company; and
(5) Banks, insurance companies, mutual funds, business development companies and SBICs, and certain employee benefit plans.

No general advertising or public solicitation is permitted, and notices must be sent to the SEC for *any* private offering, whether exempt under Rule 506 or another rule under Regulation D or under Section 4(6) as described in item d. The required notices must be sent to the SEC on Form D (1) within fifteen days after the first sale, (2) each six months after the first sale and prior to the last sale, and (3) within thirty days after the last sale.

c. A *"Rule 505" exemption*. This exemption is closely similar to the Rule 506 exemption except that
(1) the offeror cannot be a mutual fund or investment company,
(2) a $5 million ceiling applies to the aggregate amount of securities that may be issued on an exempt basis within one year,

      (3) the thirty-five-person limit does not have to include sophisticated purchasers exclusively, and

      (4) the company must not have engaged in certain prohibited conduct within the last five years. (Again, there is no limit at all on offers or sales to accredited investors.) While most blue-sky statutes of the various states have private offering exemptions parallel to the federal exemptions, few of these statutes adopt the "Rule 505" exemption, and therefore the use of this protection is usually not advisable.

   d. A *"Section 4(6)" offering.* This exemption is closely similar to the Rule 505 exemption except that

      (1) offers can *only* be made to accredited investors,

      (2) the issuer can be a mutual fund or investment company, and

      (3) there is no disqualification for prior conduct.

   e. A *"Rule 504" offering.* This exemption is similar to the Rule 505 exemption except that

      (1) the annual ceiling limitation is $500,000,

      (2) there is no disqualification for prior conduct, and

      (3) the limitation as to thirty-five offerees or purchasers does not apply.

   5. Exemption under the 1933 Act means exemption from its registration requirements. In order to protect a registration-exempt offering under the antifraud provisions of the 1933 Act, as well as under other federal and state laws and case decisions, it is advisable to prepare numbered offering packages, including an offering letter, circular, or prospectus, to conform that accurate representations were made only to identified parties meeting the legal standards for sophistication, accreditation, or other standing as lawful purchasers.

12.09 The Public Challenge

Suppose that, for whatever reason, you can't take advantage of the intrastate or private offering exemptions. Then you may need to consider a registered public offering in order to secure certain advantages. For example:

► Going public can yield vast sums of cash for all kinds of purposes, across the spectrum of any plans you have for research and development, expansion, diversification, refinancing, or other use of capital.

► Future financing may be facilitated. An initial offering will typically improve your corporate net worth and borrowing power, and the creation of a public market with decent performance in the continuing aftermarket can pave the way for issuing additional common stock or other equity capital.

► A publicly held company can acquire other companies for its own securities without depleting its cash.

► The attraction and retention of key personnel can be aided by offering stock and stock-option opportunities in a publicly held company.

► The public ownership of your company will enhance its prestige, and your important consumers and suppliers may become shareholders, more convinced than ever about your future growth.

► Your once illiquid investment in your business will be highly liquid, and perhaps more valuable than you ever dreamed.

On the other hand:

► Going public is expensive, and being a publicly held company is expensive. The legal and accounting fees for proxy materials, annual reports to shareholders, and the necessary SEC filings may cost over $100,000 annually—not counting the demand on your time and that of the other executives. There are also fees of the transfer agent, registrar, and public relations consultant, as well as the cost of your time devoted to shareholder relations.

► Going public will require prior and ongoing disclosure of your salary, corporate transactions with management, and any potential conflicts of interest. Rarely, however, will the disclosure of profits, operating procedures, and important contracts place a company at a competitive disadvantage, as management sometimes fears.

▶ There is a real possibility of loss of control. Voting trusts and multiple classes of stock may mitigate the effects of dilution, but, in the long run, management control may nonetheless be eroded.

▶ Should your company go public, anticipate a loss in decision-making flexibility too. Your compensation will be critically scrutinized, and opportunities that come your way may, of necessity, become corporate opportunities—opportunities that may need decision approval before your company can act.

▶ Officers and directors of publicly held corporations are subject to increasing personal liability for self-dealing and other conflicts of interest, for failure to exercise due diligence (section 11.06), or for negligence. Indemnification or insurance cannot fully cover this exposure (see Chapter 11).

▶ The management of a publicly held company may be preoccupied with the consequences of its decisions on the day-to-day market price of corporate stock. Thus, an R&D program may be wrongly scrapped, since it reduces short-term profits, even though it may boost long-term growth.

▶ For the sake of public appeal, a public company may pay dividends to its shareholders—taxable to you—while now, as a privately held business under your exclusive control, dividends are being kept to a minimum or avoided altogether.

▶ In its ultimate valuation of your public stock for estate tax purposes, the IRS will consider its market price. The result: certainly a higher valuation than would apply to the same stock were the business privately owned.

12.10   What Do You Have to Offer?

In weighing the positives against the negatives, evaluate yourself too. Your eligibility for public financing will depend on your sales and earnings (as compared with industry trends), the adequacy of your current and projected working capital and cash-flow levels, the quality of your management, and the future your business faces. As soon as you conclude that going public is the next logical step for your business, seek help. With the counsel of your lawyer, your accountant, and your banker, find the best managing underwriter you can.

Once selected, your underwriter may form a syndicate, commit to purchase all the securities you offer, and then resell what he can to the general public; or, more commonly, he may act as your agent and use his best efforts to sell your offering to the general public for a fee of from 7 to 10 percent of the proceeds.

First, though, your underwriter will advise and assist you in engineering the most intense metamorphosis your business will ever undergo.

The Preliminaries

Going public will be preceded by months of internal preparation, including a corporate reorganization (and often a recapitalization), a restructuring of titles to real estate, a rearrangement of permitted insiders' agreements (including stock option and other privileges), a rewriting of the corporate charter and bylaws, and a general revamping of most financial arrangements.

These, of course, presume the give-and-take decisions about the type, number, and price of securities to be sold. Frequently, at least 500,000 common shares are offered at $10 each, wisely underpriced to ensure a favorable aftermarket. However, if less than $4 million of capital is being raised, it is usually considered more advantageous to reduce the per-share price from $10 than to reduce the number of shares below 400,000.

The Registration

The Securities Act of 1933 requires any company making a public offering to disclose accurately and fully all pertinent information about the company and its offering. Although the SEC, which enforces the 1933 Act, demands comprehensive disclosure, it will not pass judgment on the merits of the company or the security. Compliance with the Act requires the filing of a two-part registration statement consisting of the prospectus and supplementary information. *

A prospectus is a disclosure document designed to inform the Commission and any prospective buyer about the structure, history, finances, and dealings of your company, and about the nature of your proposed offering in a literal, formalized manner. At the same time, the prospectus serves as an advertising document to induce offerees to buy. And so a balance must be struck between conservatism and optimism. The prospectus must neither misrepresent nor mislead, and conservatism must triumph—even to the point of highlighting adverse factors including operating losses, dependence on key suppliers or customers, conflicts of interest, and increasing industry regulation.

Supplementary information includes financial statements and detailed information about past offerings in a question-and-answer format. Supplementary information is not distributed publicly, but it is open for public inspection at the Commission's offices and thus is available to sophisticated investors.

The Waiting Period

After the registration statement is filed, expect to wait several months until it becomes effective. In the interim, the Commission will review your statement and may issue a letter of comment (or a deficiency letter), seeking more facts or a revision in your prospectus. During your statement's pendency, securities may not be sold, but they may be described in "tombstone" ads, word-of-mouth pitches, and preliminary prospectus ("red herring") mailings. "Indications of interest" may be accepted from would-be buyers, but actual sales may not yet be consummated, nor may offers to buy or sell be issued.

---

* Regulation A allows a short-form, "baby" registration for offerings not exceeding $1 million. Not only does Regulation A provide a simpler and cheaper way to go public, it may be quicker: Baby registrations are filed at easily accessible regional SEC offices.

The Effective Date

Congratulations! You are now free to sell your securities. And you are now bond to disclose publicly and promptly all material developments—good or bad—that might affect the value of your securities. You are obliged to refrain from trading on inside information until it is publicly disclosed, and you are prohibited from selling your controlling shares except in the manner and to the extent the law will allow. Should your publicly held company have assets in excess of $3 million and more than 500 shareholders (or should its stock be listed on a stock exchange), you will be subject to the additional registration requirements of the Securities Act of 1934. These include annual (Form 10K), quarterly (Form 10Q), and special (Form 8K) disclosures; special rules relating to the solicitation of proxies, insider reporting, and accountability for short-term profits by directors, officers, and 10 percent shareholders; and tender-offer reporting.

12.11   Success at Last

A well-planned public offering must result from a long-range study under the guidance of your attorney, who will eventually recruit the brainpower of a top-flight securities attorney. Yet going public is not always a necessary move in the growth of a profitable business; nor, as we have seen, is it always wise. Entertaining a public offering and its alternatives is merely one sign that you have achieved a measure of success and fulfillment that others may rightfully envy.

Glossary

accrual-basis accounting A method of accounting reflecting income and expense for a given time period that is based on the right to receive the income, or the obligation to pay the expense, even though the income is not actually received, or the expense is not actually paid, during such period.

blue-sky laws State laws regulating the sale of securities and offers to sell and regulating the parties connected with sales and offers of securities, such as issuers, underwriters, broker-dealers, and investment advisers.

Bulk Sales Act A federal or state law designed to protect creditors when a business is sold in a single transaction or in a series of actions that are related so as to be the equivalent of a single transaction.

cash-basis accounting A method of accounting reflecting income and expense for a given time period that is based on the actual receipt of income, or the actual payment of expense, even though the right to receive the income, or the obligation to pay the expense, does not arise during such period.

closely held corporation A corporation the stock of which is held by a small number of shareholders, with fifteen being a number set out in many state laws—subject to variation.

Fed, the The Federal Reserve Board, an independent federal agency that regulates members of the Federal Reserve System, which members include most U.S. banks.

horizontal combination   An arrangement between or among companies that operate *at the same level* in the producer-to-consumer sequence, such levels usually proceeding from producers to distributors, next to wholesalers, and then to retailers, but sometimes, as in the case of the gasoline industry, skipping over one or more of the intermediary levels.

1934 Exchange Act   The Securities Exchange Act of 1934, a federal statute (15 USC §§ 78a *et seq.*).

1933 Act   The Securities Act of 1933, a federal statute (15 USC §§ 77a *et seq.*).

public corporation   A corporation set up by law to serve as a subdivision or agency of the federal or a state or local government.

tender offer   A publicly made offer to acquire securities of a company for an amount in cash or other consideration that is described in the offer. There is usually a time limit on the duration of the offer, a requirement that a specified minimum amount of securities be submitted (or "tendered") for acceptance by the offeror, and other conditions.

vertical combination   An arrangement between or among companies that operate *at different levels* in the producer-to-consumer sequence, such levels usually proceeding from producers to distributors, next to wholesalers, and then to retailers, but sometimes, as in the case of the gasoline industry, skipping over one or more of the intermediary levels.

Acronyms

ADS The alternative depreciation system, a straight-line system for computing depreciation deductions over time periods set out in the Internal Revenue Code for each class of property and subject to a year-by-year election of a taxpayer as to each depreciable asset.

AMT The alternative minimum tax, a federal income tax imposed on all taxpayers except partnerships and S corporations.

AMTI Alternative minimum taxable income, regular taxable income under the Internal Revenue Code, but after such regular income is increased or reduced by required adjustments.

CPA A certified public accountant, an accountant who meets the training and testing standards of a recognized organization.

D&O Director(s) and officer(s) of one or more corporations.

EDA The Economic Development Administration, an agency of the United States Department of Commerce.

EEO The Equal Employment Opportunity Act, a federal statute (42 USC §§ 2000e *et seq.*; Title VII of the Civil Rights Act of 1964).

EEOC The United States Equal Employment Opportunity Commission, a federal commission created by the Civil Rights Act of 1964.

ERISA The Employee Retirement Income Security Act of 1974, a federal statute (Pub. Law 93-406).

ESOP   Employee stock ownership plan, a plan under which employees acquire interests in the capital stock of their employer.

FDCPA   The Fair Debt Collection Practices Act, a federal statute regulating practices by creditors in collecting obligations owed to them.

FDIC   The Federal Deposit Insurance Corporation, which insures deposits up to $100,000 in most accounts with banks.

FHLBB   The Federal Home Loan Bank Board, an independent federal agency that regulates members of the Federal Home Loan Bank, which members include most savings and loan associations and federal savings banks.

FSLIC   The Federal Savings and Loan Insurance Corporation, which insures deposits up to $100,000 in most accounts with savings and loan associations and federal savings banks.

ISO   An incentive stock option, an option meeting requirements set out in the Internal Revenue Code and granting the right to purchase stock of a corporation.

IRA   Individual retirement account, a tax-favored form of investment account that is subject to penalties for withdrawals prior to age 59.

MACRS   The modified accelerated cost recovery system, a method described in the Internal Revenue Code for claiming tax deductions for depreciation of property.

MBDA   The Minority Business Development Agency, a federal agency designed to assist the development of minority businesses.

NLRB   The National Labor Relations Board, an independent federal agency that oversees the fairness of negotiations between labor unions and businesses and other areas of such employment relationships.

NOL   Net operating loss, a tax deduction for a business loss that usually can be carried three years back or fifteen years forward under the Internal Revenue Code.

OSHA   The Occupational Safety and Health Act, a federal statute (29 USC §§ 651 *et seq.*) or the Occupational Safety and Health Administration, a federal agency created by the aforementioned statute to regulate safe practices in the workplace.

P&L   Profit and loss, usually referring to an accounting report for an organization's activities over a period of time.

QJSA   Qualified joint and survivor annuity, a form of retirement benefit for married participants in most employee retirement and profit-sharing plans.

QPSA   Qualified preretirement survivor annuity, an annuity payable to the surviving spouse of a participant in a retirement or profit-sharing plan who dies prior to retirement but after reaching an age at which retirement benefits could have started.

REIT   Real estate investment trust, a trust designed to hold investments in real property. The REIT is taxed only on income not distributed to beneficiaries provided it meets requirements described in the Internal Revenue Code.

SBA   The Small Business Administration, a federal agency that provides financial and other assistance to businesses of limited size, to the extent of congressional appropriations of funds.

SBIC   Small business investment company, a company that may qualify for tax benefits under the Internal Revenue Code provided the losses result from investments in small businesses.

SCORE   The Service Corps of Retired Executives, a volunteer organization affiliated with the SBA that provides management counseling and training to small businesses.

TIL   The Truth-in-Lending Act, a federal statute (15 USC §§ 1601 *et seq.*).

UCC   The Uniform Commercial Code, a model statute proposed by the Commission on Uniform Laws and adopted, with substantial variations, in forty-nine states (Louisiana excepted).

UCCC   The Uniform Consumer Credit Code, a model statute proposed by the Commission on Uniform Laws and adopted in several states.

Index

247